A fine dining approach to God's own cuisine: Kerala

Beyond Curry
Fine Dining Indian Cuisine Series

Dedication

I dedicate this effort to my father, the late Shri. Padmanabha Pillai Retnakumar.

Work done for www.finediningindian.com

All contents copyright 2013 by bobby retnakumar geetha. All rights reserved. No part of this document or the related files may be reproduced or transmitted in any form, by any means (electronic, photocopying, recording, or otherwise) without the prior written permission of publisher.

Limit of liability and disclaimer of warranty: the publisher has used its best efforts in preparing this book, and the information provided herein is provided "as is." bobby retnakumar geetha makes no representation or warranties with respect to the accuracy or completeness of the contents of this book and specifically disclaims any implied warranties of merchantability or fitness for any particular purpose and shall in no event be liable for any loss of profit or any other commercial damage, including but not limited to special, incidental, consequential, or other damages.

Copyright © 2013 bobby retnakumar geetha
All rights reserved.

About finediningindian.com

finediningindian.com was created to represent fine dining Indian cuisine to the world as a pioneer and strong contender to be one of the top cuisines in the world. We intend to support great innovations in Indian cooking so that it will gain worldwide popularity. We plan to achieve this by developing new cooking techniques and positive eating habits through Indian cuisine.

All these developments we will bring forward by keeping all authenticity of our great cuisine and cultural integration with it.

Our vision

To be the leader in inspiring and developing a new generation of Indian cuisine and chefs.

Contents

Acknowledgments 6

Kerala and Its Amazing Cuisine 11

Kerala Cuisine Ingredients 19

Cooking and Preserving Methods in Kerala 32

Utensils Used in Kerala Home Cooking 38

Food Design Concepts 41

Starting Your Own Restaurant 53

Poultry Recipes 61

Seafood Recipes 81

Red Meat Recipes 101

Vegetable Recipes 115

Staple Recipes 132

Pickles and Condiments 160

Online Resources 171

Acknowledgments

My sincere thanks go to my wife, Supriya, for providing the necessary research and editorial support, to my mother, Geetha, for inspiring me to cook through her culinary skills in my early childhood, and to my brother, Arun, for his love and support.

My heartfelt respect goes to teachers from my school, culinary instructors from college days at IHM Thiruvananthapuram, Kerala, and my senior chefs in all levels, from whom I gained my cooking knowledge. For my friends in all stages of my life, I remember all their contributions and support in my career. To name a few: Ms. Padmakumari, Chef Rajshekar, Chef Pradosh Pai, Chef Sony Haq, Chef Ivan Thomas, Mr. Premchand, Chef Natrajan Kulandai, Chef Arzooman Irani, Chef Philippe Maratier, Chef Robert Cauchi, Chef Andy Brookes, Chef Kunj Kashyap, Chef Vincent Menager.

With great regards and respect,

Bobby retnakumar geetha

Introduction

As a proud Indian and chef, I have a moral duty to give back what I got from my teachers through sharing my knowledge with my juniors, so that they don't have to start from where I started rather than from where I reached. That will help my fellow chefs conquer greater heights for the benefit of Indian cuisine.

As far as I am concerned, Indian cuisine has much more to offer than is perceived internationally. I'd like to share a few good recipes from my mother and to show our chefs the way to plate Indian food in a fine dining style without altering original style.

I would love to prove a point that all budding chefs have their own individuality,Keep encouraging your own style, and write down your experiments so that one day you can also publish your own cookbook.

 I believe this book is one of my life's purposes. I hope to bring a change in the way we cook and present Indian food.

 In order to start, I decided to focus on the flavorful Kerala cuisine, my home cuisine.

Later, I intend to research other great Indian cuisines and reveal their potential to the world one by one.

We have a great cuisine with amazing regional variations. We do not have to copy other cuisines in order to achieve modernity.

Our cooking methods are so strong and diverse when fully used for the benefit of each ingredient; Indian cuisine is the best in all standards in the modern kitchen.

I remember a question I was asked on my campus interview for a management trainee position in one of the prestigious hotel companies in India: "Why you want to specialize in Indian cuisine, and what do you want to do?"

The answer got me my first job: "I strongly believe Indian cuisine is the only cuisine you cannot get the original taste without experiencing the authentic dish, and cannot replicate by reading the recipe.

The changes I want to bring to Indian cuisine are simple cooking methods, simple recipes, and positive eating habits."

Through the book I'd like to influence my great Indian chefs in presenting dishes to an international platform where chefs in other countries should be inspired by our cuisine.

If I can inspire one of you to come up with a culinary manual of your own cooking style, then my objective is fulfilled

No other country in the world is categorized as independent ruling states through the languages people speak. Each state has its own customs and culinary heritage.

As a first step, I'll discuss with you my home state—Kerala.Kerala cuisine is a hidden gem of Indian culinary heritage.

Kerala is a southern state of India and is advertised by state tourism as "God's own country" for its natural beauty.

When considering international recognition for Indian cuisine, Kerala has not yet received its deserved place.

As a chef I am proud to represent my homeland. In this book the basic recipes are preserved in their original forms from my mother, even when presented in a luxurious way.

This book is done more as a chef-learning diary than a normal cookbook; all the recipes are tested and tried in my home kitchen.

Through the book, I would like to share more than Kerala and its cuisine. We will discuss food design, plating concepts, the restaurant business, and being a restaurant owner.

"Dear chefs: Have the dream to open your own food business while working for someone"

Kerala and Its Amazing Cuisine

Kerala or Keralam is an Indian state located on the Malabar Coast of southwest India. Thiruvanthapuram is the state capital. Malayalam is the main language, but English is also understood by the majority of Keralites.

Kerala cuisine is an unexplored area of Indian cuisine. Its possibilities are unlimited and very cost-effective in terms of producing fantastic dishes. Kerala dishes are simple and lean compared to other rich cuisines of India, mainly due to the coastal influence in Kerala cuisine.
Kerala cuisine has a fantastic legacy of seafood recipes, which will be an added advantage for any Indian restaurant.

Kerala cuisine has to be marketed to bring in clients since it is a different taste from the normal Indian cuisine. Kerala is India's top tourist destination and is famous for beaches, backwaters, cuisine, hill resorts, yoga, and Ayurveda treatments. The Kerala tourism board branded the state as "God's own country." It lives up to the brand image and is now one of the best destinations in the Asian Pacific.

Beyond curry by bobby

Kerala may not be popular around the globe, but the world kitchens cannot be complete without spices exported from India.

Kerala's history is closely linked with its commerce, which until recent times revolved around its spice trade. Celebrated as the spice coast of India, ancient Kerala played host to travellers and traders from across the world, including the Greeks, Romans, Arabs, Chinese, Portuguese, Dutch, French, and British. Almost all of them have left their imprint on this land in some form or another—architecture, cuisine, or literature.

Kerala is a land of multicultural and religious communities where each community in the state celebrates its own festivals.

There are some festivals unique to the state of Kerala. Most important of them are Onam and Vishu.

Onam is a traditional harvest festival of Kerala. This falls in the months of August to September. The festival is meant to celebrate the annual homecoming of the king Mahabali.

The festival happens for ten days, and colorful carpet is laid in front of every house during these days. Families serve a traditional meal called "sadhya" during this time, especially on the ninth and tenth days. The meal is served in the traditional way in banana leaves with around twenty to twenty-eight dishes.

Vishu is the traditional new year's day of the state and is another traditional festival occasion for Kerala. Vishu has a lot of significance for Hindus, as Vishu marks the astronomical New Year. People believe that Vishu is the festival that brings prosperity and calm to life.

This festival falls in the month of April and is considered the most auspicious day of the year. Even on this day, a traditional meal or sadhya is prepared by the women of the house, and the whole family has the lunch together.

Kerala Cuisine

Kerala food is moderately spicy in nature, but most flavorful, and its recipes promote locally grown ingredients for cooking.

Kerala is the home of kera known as the coconut tree. Coconut is the base for many dishes and is used in almost every dish in Kerala. Coconut oil is used for cooking. The oil is extracted from the dried coconut or "kopra." Grated coconut and coconut milk are widely used in dishes for thickening and flavoring.

Rice and tapioca (cassava) are the most common foods of Kerala. Varieties of main dishes are made with these two. Seafood is also one of the very famous foods. Fish, crab, shellfish, lobster, and prawn are used for everyday cooking. Sardines and mackerel are the most commonly used varieties of fish.

The different meat varieties used in Kerala kitchens include poultry, red meats, and a few game birds (now restricted by law).

Kerala breakfast shows a rich variety. Most of the breakfast dishes are made from rice flour. Some of the breakfast dishes are appam, idiyappam, idli, dosa, and puttu. Along with this, some of the side dishes are made with coconut.

For lunch and dinner, the main dish is boiled rice. Along with this, there will be one or more curries and side dishes. There are several varieties of vegetarian and nonvegetarian curries and side dishes.

Popular vegetarian dishes are sambar, rasam, aviyal, kaalan, olan, erisherry, pulisherry, thoran, pachadi, and kichadi.

Food in Kerala is generally steamed and lightly tempered. Most of the dishes are spicy. Non-vegetarian dishes include chicken, fish, and lamb. Curry, fry, and ullarthu are made from these varieties.

Nowadays, Kerala people often have chapattis or food made of wheat, especially for dinner. Grains like ragi and millet are common in some parts of south India.

Onasadhya

Kerala is famous for its traditional banquet called "sadhya." This is a vegetarian meal served with boiled rice as the main dish and along with variety of side dishes. This traditional meal is prepared during special occasions and festivals and is served in a banana leaf.

Kerala cuisine and the eating habits of its people are closely related to its festivals, especially Onam. A proper sadhya is the traditional vegetarian feast of Kerala. Usually served as lunch, it consists of parboiled pink rice, side dishes, savouries, pickles, and desserts spread out on a plantain leaf. Tradition insists that the tapered end of the leaf points to the left of the seated guest. Rice is served on the lower half of the leaf. The feast begins with the serving of parippu, a lentil preparation made of small gram and ghee.

The second course is sambar, the famous south Indian vegetable stew in which any available combination of vegetables is boiled in a gravy of crushed lentils, onions, chilies, coriander, and turmeric, with a pinch of asafetida.

Avial, an essential side dish, is a blend of vegetables, cconut paste, and green chilies. Some of the other important side dishes include thoran and olan. Thoran can be minced string beans, cabbage, radish, or grams, mixed with grated coconut and sautéed with a dash of red chilies and turmeric powder. Olan is a bland dish of pumpkin and red gram cooked in a thin gravy of coconut milk.

The savouries include upperi, pappadum, ginger pickle, pachadi, and kichadi. Upperi is deep-fried banana chips. Pappadums are fried, creamy yellow, sun-dried wafers of black gram flour. The ginger pickle is a rich brown, hot, and sweet ginger chutney, while the kichadi consists of sliced and sautéed cucumber or ladyfingers in curd, seasoned with mustard, red chilies, and curry leaves in coconut oil. Pickles are usually mango and lime.

Desserts are served midway through the meal. The payasam is a thick, fluid dish of sweet brown molasses, coconut milk, and spices, garnished with cashew nuts and raisins.

There could be a succession of payasams, such as the palada pradhaman and parippu pradhaman. Pazham, a small, ripe, golden-yellow plantain, is usually eaten with the payasams.

After the payasams, rice is served once more with the spicy rasam. Rasam is a mixture of chili and peppercorn powders boiled in diluted tamarind juice. Kaalan, seasoned buttermilk with turmeric powder and green chilies, and plain sour buttermilk that comes salted and with chopped green chilies and ginger, are served before the feast is finally wound up.

Seasons of Kerala

Constantly pleasant and equable in climate throughout the year, Kerala is a tropical land with the coast running down its entire length and the western Ghats forming a protective barrier against the dry winds from up north.

The main seasons are monsoon (June to November) and summer (February to May), while winter is only a slight drop in temperature from the normal range of 28–32 °C.

Seasons have a great impact on the farming community of Kerala. Almost thirty years ago, the main occupation of Kerala was farming, including rice, coconut, spices, tapioca, banana, and many tropical fruits and vegetables.

Kerala cuisine ingredients

Spices, defined as strongly flavored and aromatic substances obtained from plants in seed, leaf, bud, or flower form, form an integral part of Kerala cooking. In ancient times, spices were as precious as gold and diamonds. India produces many kinds of spices, and most quality spices come from Kerala. Spices are considered good for our taste buds and health. The commonly used spices are cumin, green chili, coriander, cinnamon, clove, cardamom, pepper, dried red chili, curry leaf, coriander leaf, ginger, garlic, mustard seeds, and asafetida.

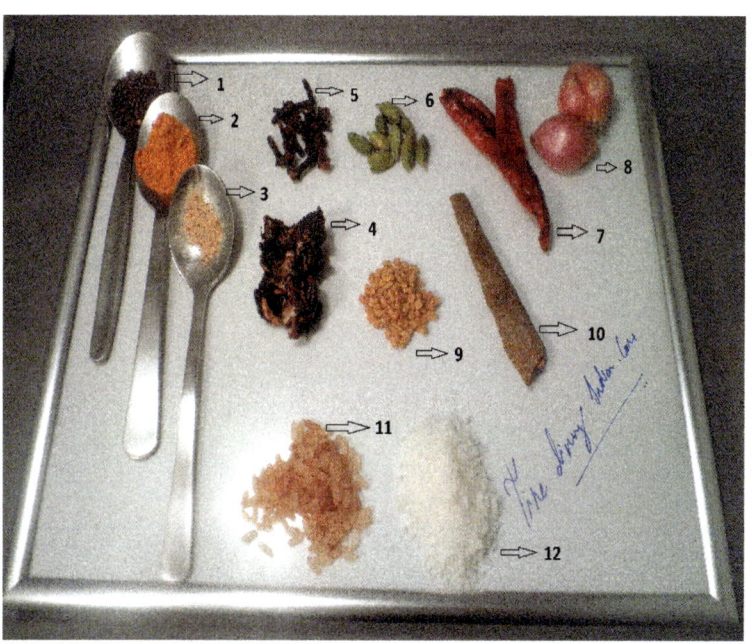

1. Mustard seed
2. Turmeric
3. Asafoetida
4. Tamarind
5. Cloves
6. Cardamom
7. Chilly
8. Shallots/Sambar Onion
9. Fenugreek
10. Cinnamon
11. Brown Rice
12. Coconut grated

Pepper

Pepper has been grown and used in Indian cuisine, and specifically in Kerala cuisine, since 2000 BC. Europeans and westerners came to India only due to the presence of pepper.

Pepper is considered the black gold. India and Vietnam are the largest producers of pepper.

Pepper mainly comes in two forms, black and white. Black is produced by lightly cooking the unripe pepper with the skin and then drying it. White is the seed of pepper with the skin removed.

Cardamom

Cardamom is the most easily recognizable sweet spice and is grown on the hillsides of Kerala. It is the world's third-most-expensive spice by weight, outstripped in market value by only saffron and vanilla.

Cardamom has a strong, unique taste, with an intensely aromatic, resinous fragrance.

Black cardamom has a distinctly more smoky, though not bitter, aroma with a coolness some consider similar to mint. **Green** cardamom is one of the most expensive spices by weight, but little is needed to impart the flavor.Cardamom is best stored in pod form because once the seeds are exposed or ground, they quickly lose their flavor. Cardamom belongs to the ginger family Zingiberaceae.

Cinnamon

Cinnamon is a very important spice in any Kerala meat preparation and the spice blend "garam masala," which is different from the one used in north India.It's obtained from the inner bark of several trees from the genus Cinnamomum that are cultivated on the hills of Kerala.

Cloves

Cloves are grown in mountain areas of Kerala. They are used in cooking either completely or in a ground form, but as they are extremely strong, they are used sparingly.

Cloves are the aromatic dried flower buds of a tree in the family Myrtaceae.

The clove tree is an evergreen that grows to a height ranging from 8–12 m, having large leaves and reddish brown flowers in numerous groups of terminal clusters.

The flower buds are at first pale in color and gradually become green, after which they develop into a bright red when they are ready for collecting.

Fenugreek

Fenugreek is the small, cube-shaped, yellow seeds of fenugreek plant. Both the seeds and plant are used for cooking.

Fenugreek when sautéed in oil produces an excellent fragrance that is common to Indian curries. In Kerala cuisine, fenugreek seeds are more often used than the plants.

Most Kerala fish dishes are enriched with the flavor of fenugreek seeds, which masks the unpleasant fishy smell.

Mustard Seeds

Widely used for the preparation of dishes in Kerala, mustard seeds are the small, round seeds of various mustard plants. The seeds are usually about 1 or 2 mm in diameter. There are three main varieties of mustard. Mustard seeds grow well in temperate regions. Mustard is considered to be a rich source of oil and protein. Seeds are available as whole seeds, split seeds, or powder and paste. It's ideal to store mustard seeds in a clean and dry container or jar, because they form clumps when wet. Mustard is used in the tempering of spices. The procedure of heating oil, dropping in mustard seeds, and cooking them until they pop gives many dishes a distinctive flavor. However, mustard is really a preservative, and the seeds are used for pickling in most Kerala households.

Chilies

There is rarely any Kerala food without chilies in it. Chilies are fruits of the capsicum species. They are cultivated mainly in tropical and subtropical countries.India is the largest producer and exporter of chilies. Ripe chilies, which are red in color, are picked from the plant and dried in the sun.

Fresh, unripe chilies come in various shades of green, and they are better for flavor. Both red and green chilies come from the same plant, it is just that the peppers change color as they ripen, and they have a strong aroma. Chilies are available fresh, dried, powdered, and flaked.

Curry Leaf

Curry leaf comes from a beautiful tree called the curry tree, which grows well in tropical climates and is native to India. Curry leaf is present in almost each dish in Kerala. As the tree is widely grown, the leaves are inexpensive. Curry leaves are available fresh and dried. They are dropped into hot oil that is then poured on top of many dishes to add flavor. While they add their lingering aroma to a dish, they are normally not eaten by people.

Tamarind

The tamarind tree is an evergreen, long-lived, medium-growth, bushy tree. Its fruit is called the tamarind pod. It has a crescent shape and is brown with a thin, brittle shell.

It contains a fleshy pulp. When it is mature, the flesh is colored brown or reddish brown. Within this pulp, there is a seed, which is dark brown in color. The pulp is used as flavoring for its sweet, sour taste and is said to be high in acid, sugar, vitamin B, and calcium. It is available as a pressed fibrous slab or concentrated paste. Tamarind extract is used in some dishes, especially in fish curries, to give a sweet-and-sour flavor to the curry. Tamarind slabs and paste store well and will last for up to a year.

Kokum

Kokum is native to India and is endemic to the western coastal regions of south India. The kokum tree is of tropical evergreen origin. It is a sour fruit that resembles tamarind. Kokum is deep purple in color when ripe and has large seeds. The fruits are pickled when ripe. The rind is then removed and soaked repeatedly in the juice of the pulp and then dried under the sun. The rind is used as the flavoring for food. It has a sweet-and-sour taste and gives a purple color to the food.

Tapioca

Tapioca is the fully grown root of the tapioca plant. The name is derived from the cassava or yuca plant. It is often used to thicken soups and sweeten the flavor of the food. Kerala is one of the few states in India that use tapioca as a staple food. Tapioca is gluten-free and almost completely protein-free. In Kerala, tapioca is the best combination meal along with a spicy fish curry. I have provided the recipe in the last chapter.

Kerala Banana

The two most famous Kerala banana varieties are plantain (large, yellow banana) and red banana. Red is a variety of banana with reddish-purple skin and is smaller than other bananas. In comparison to other bananas, the red banana is sweeter and softer. The redder the fruit, the more taste. It is also higher in vitamin C. Red bananas are eaten in the same way as yellow bananas, and they are available year-round. Plantain is used in many forms in Kerala cuisine.

The famous Kerala chip is made from plantain. Numerous sweets and savories are also made from plantain. Raw plantain is good for making crisps.

Banana Flower and Stem
The flower is taken only after the banana has grown to its full volume and is often used in Kerala cooking as a source for the main vegetarian dish enriched with high nutritional value. The banana stem, which is white, is the innermost part. It looks similar to palm heart and is treated the same as the banana flower. Both will oxidize faster if not kept in water after cutting.

Brown Rice

Also called part-milled rice, brown rice is a whole, natural grain. It is more nutritious than white rice. This rice is now more expensive because of its low supply and difficulty of storage. Brown rice has a shelf life of approximately six to seven months.

In Kerala rice is a staple, and most families use brown rice.

Colacasia (Chembu)

Colacasia is a tuber of which both leaves and root are used for cooking. The plant is called "elephant ears" due to its large size. Colacasia is an integral part of sambar, the very famous Kerala dish that is necessary in all vegetarian feasts. Colacasia has a high starch content and a sticky nature. It is good for sautéing or stir-frying with an addition of grated coconut.

Yam (Chena)

Another tuber, the yam is very common in Kerala; its stem and root are used for cooking. Unlike colacasia, the root is hard and requires long cooking. Yam is best for stewing. It can also be used for stir-frying, but pre-cooking is advised.

Coconut

The name Kerala originated from "kera," or coconut tree, and coconut is termed as "nalikeram." Kerala cooking is not complete without coconut. Coconut is used mainly in three forms: grated coconut, coconut milk, and coconut oil.

Kerala dishes will not be authentic if you do not use coconut oil in cooking, according to studies made by the coconut board of the Indian government.

Asafetida

Asafetida is extracted from the root of perennial plant, which is native to Afghanistan and imported to India .The plant is a species of ferula and looks similar to fennel. Asafetida is mainly sold in two forms: solid cake and powdered. In olden days, Kerala households used solid asafetida diluted in lukewarm water. The raw flavor of asafetida is unpleasant, but heating it with oil or ghee (clarified butter) gives it a very appetizing flavor.

Jackfruit

Jackfruit is the largest tree-borne fruit and is grown extensively in the tropical climate region. Archaeological surveys in India have found jackfruit cultivation as far back as three thousand to six thousand years. In Kerala cuisine, jackfruit is used in both its raw and ripened forms. Varieties are distinguished according to the characteristics of the fruit's flesh.

Drumstick

Drumstick is taken from the drumstick tree. It is an exceptionally nutritious vegetable tree with a variety of potential uses. Drumstick is the most commonly used vegetable in Kerala. It is a main ingredient in curries and side dishes like sambar, theeyal, and thoran.Drumstick and its leaves are widely available in Kerala and there is at least one tree in almost every house in Kerala.Drumstick is helpful in increasing breast milk in the breastfeeding months. It is also believed to have great aphrodisiac properties.

Toddy

Toddy is an alcoholic beverage taken from the sap of the coconut tree or palm tree. It is a traditional beverage of Kerala with a long history. Toddy is collected in a mud pot from the unbloomed flower pod of the coconut or palm tree. The pot is taken in the morning or evening, where morning is sweet and evening tends to be more alcoholic since it is allowed to ferment.

Toddy was traditionally used to ferment rice to make appam (hoppers). Now yeast is used instead.

Coconut Oil

Coconut oil is extracted from dried coconuts and is commonly used in cooking. It gives flavor to the dishes. Coconut oil has a smoking point of 138 °C. Coconut oil has a fairly long shelf life of about two years because of its natural saturated fat content.

Mustard Oil

Mustard oil is extracted from mustard seeds. The oil can be extracted from black, brown, and white mustards. In Kerala, mustard oil often used for pickling.The oil is heated before cooking to reduce the strong smell and taste. Mustard seeds have high levels of omega-3. Mustard oil is also used for Ayurveda massages to improve blood circulation.

Gingelly Oil

Gingelly oil is also known as sesame oil. It is an edible vegetable oil extracted from sesame seeds and is used in some Kerala dishes such as dosa and idli.This oil is perfect for deep-frying and can be used for stir-frying meats and vegetables. Hindus use gingelly oil to light oil lamps for God. Gingelly oil is a source of vitamins.

Cooking and Preserving Methods in Kerala Cuisine

Kerala cuisine is blessed with some fantastic cooking methods that have been carefully designed for the maximum utilization of natural resources. I have described our traditional cooking methods in terms of international cooking styles. Therefore, I may not use traditional wording, but the result is the same. Kerala cuisine has a great tradition of vegetarian cuisine related to Hinduism. Most of the vegetarian dishes are slow cooked and require boiling, stewing, or a combination of these methods.

With the influence of other non-Hindu communities in Kerala, some excellent non-vegetarian recipes came to exist./
The traders who came to Kerala for spices brought together their cooking traditions and cooking methods. Kerala cuisine also boasts traditional methods of preserving food ingredients by pickling and drying. Pickles are the first dish served on the banana leaf for "Sadhya."

Some common cooking methods that still exist are described below.

Stewing

Stewing is a method of cooking all the ingredients together in a liquid over low heat for a relatively long period. In Kerala cuisine, most of the curries are made in this style. The cooking period depends on numerous factors, such as cuts of meat, quality of the ingredients, cooking equipment, and method adopted. Vegetables like carrots, potatoes, green peas, and tomatoes are the main ingredients for a stew.

In Kerala, most of the stewing curries are thickened naturally either by potato used in the stew or by reducing and then finishing with coconut milk. Meats such as beef, chicken, or lamb are suitable for slow cooking.

In a stew, the gravy usually covers the meat. One of the best ways is to sear the meat and vegetables before stewing. In Kerala cuisine, we have a prominent influence of Portuguese cooking, and some of the stewing methods have been adopted with few changes. Vegetable stew or ishtew is used as an accompaniment to chapatti and appam. Innovative chefs have tried preparing lamb and chicken in a similar style and had good success in those dishes.

Boiling

Boiling food in water is an ancient and traditional method used in Kerala cooking. Boiling temperature is maintained above 99 °C, and you can see the vigorous motion of the liquid on the surface. It is a very harsh technique of cooking. It is best to cook meat and root vegetables by boiling because of their hard texture. Rice and potatoes are suitable for boiling. Rice is boiled first, dried, and then partially milled to remove its husk.

In Kerala almost all tea stalls have a traditional wood-burning boiler that is heated almost twenty-four hours a day. It has multiple uses, including steaming bananas, boiling eggs, and making tea.

Frying

In frying, oil is used as the cooking medium. The food is cooked quickly and gets a crispy texture. Adjusting the oil quantity results in several different frying methods, including panfrying, deep frying, sautéing, and stir-frying. Sautéing and stir-frying are similar and use only a small amount of oil for frying on a hot surface.

For panfrying, use only the required amount of oil to immerse one third to one half of each piece of food. Deep-frying is the method of totally immersing the food in the hot oil. Deep-fried oil can be used again until the oil color changes or taste varies. Dishes used for deep-frying need a coating layer marinade for giving a crispy coating.

Steaming

Steaming is a cooking method using steam produced by boiling water. The food is not put directly into the boiling water, but is kept separate from the water using a perforated plate and is cooked by contact with the steam.

With this method, the food gets a moist texture and retains more nutrients than with boiling.

In Kerala, there is a special steamer pot. There is a wide variety of steamed food in Kerala, mainly breakfast foods, including idli, idiyappam, and kozhukatta.

Pickling

Pickling is a process of preserving food in brine or an acidic medium. Brine is a solution of salt water. A common test of brine quality involves dropping a clean, washed, raw; egg when it floats, the proportion of salt to water is ideal.

The food preserved using this method is called pickle. Pickling enhances the flavors by concentrating them.

Pickling promotes osmosis, the process of moving water molecules through a permeable membrane to a higher concentrated solution, thereby equalizing both sides.

Kerala has a large variety of pickles, including raw mango, lemon, garlic, tomato, and chili. There are non-vegetarian pickles as well.

The main fish used for pickling is tuna. Prawns are also good for pickling.

The fruits, vegetables, and fish are mixed with ingredients such as salt, spices, and mustard oil, and are set to mature. Pickled foods will last for up to a year or more.

Drying

Drying is the oldest method of preserving food and usually uses natural sunlight. The process removes all moisture from the food.

Many foods are preserved by drying and can be stored for later use.

In Kerala, fishes such as tuna, mackerel, and sardine are salted and dried. This is done mostly by the fishing community when they have a stock of fish left after the day's sale.

The fish is soaked in salt water for a couple of days and is dried in the sun. The fish can be later soaked and made into curry or powdered to make chutneys.

Dried mango is also very common in Kerala. Sliced raw mango is soaked in brine for two days and then strained and dried under the sun or in hot areas in the kitchen.

Kerala Cooking Utensils

Appa chatti: Concave pan for making appam.

Cheena chatti: Deep frying pan made of aluminium or cast iron, introduced to Kerala by China.

Dosa kallu: Cast iron griddle for making dosa (rice pancakes).

Mun chatti: Clay pot for cooking curries. Nowadays curries are also made in non-stick pans. However, clay pots are a more environmentally friendly and healthy option, and they add a distinct taste to the curry.

Puttu steamer: Special utensils for steaming roasted rice flour.

Idli/idiyappam tattu: Mould for making idli and idiyappam.

Seva nazhi: Extruder or mould for making idiyappam.

Unniappam pan: Concave pan with twelve or more slots and a 30–50 mL batter-holding capacity in each slot.

Uruli/varpu: Flat utensils best for making large-volume dishes, made with aluminium or bronze.

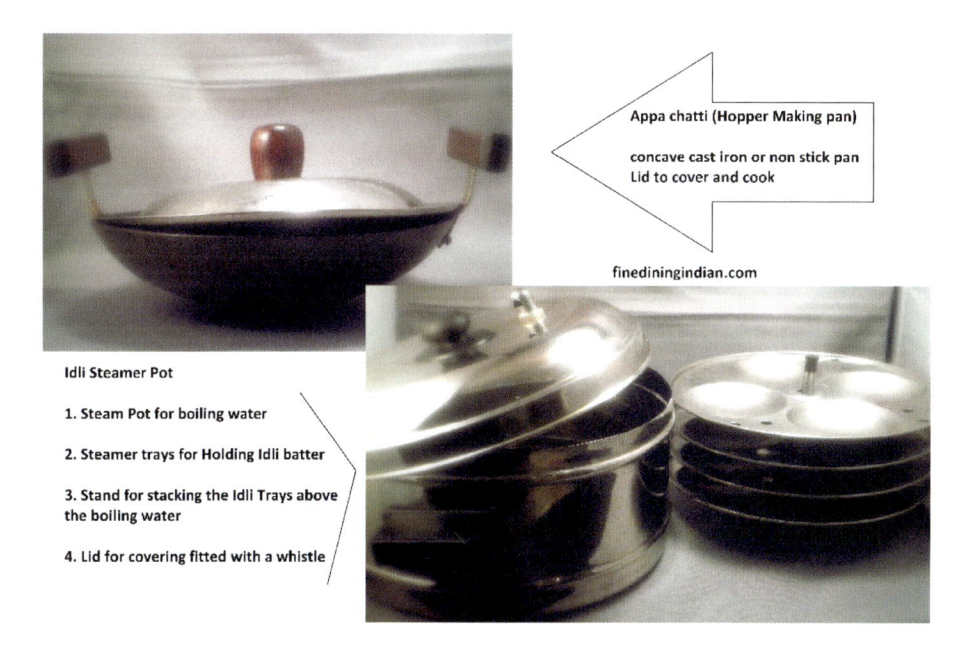

Appa chatti (Hopper Making pan)

concave cast iron or non stick pan
Lid to cover and cook

finediningindian.com

Idli Steamer Pot

1. Steam Pot for boiling water
2. Steamer trays for Holding Idli batter
3. Stand for stacking the Idli Trays above the boiling water
4. Lid for covering fitted with a whistle

Dosa Pan -
Flat round,
Made of Cast Iron or Nonstick Pan

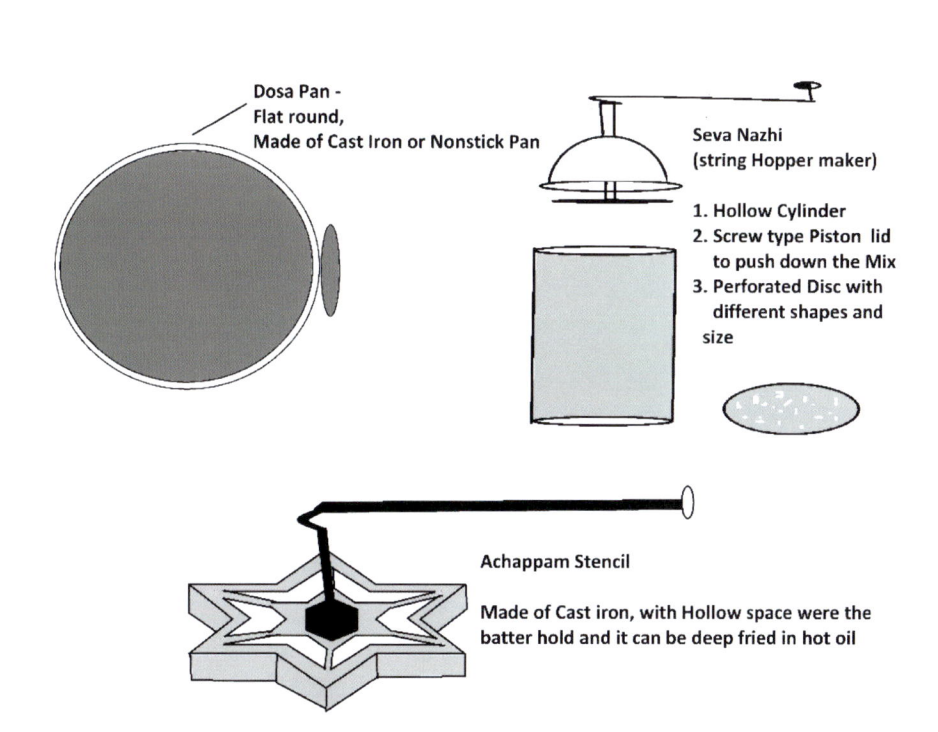

Seva Nazhi
(string Hopper maker)

1. Hollow Cylinder
2. Screw type Piston lid to push down the Mix
3. Perforated Disc with different shapes and size

Achappam Stencil

Made of Cast iron, with Hollow space were the batter hold and it can be deep fried in hot oil

39

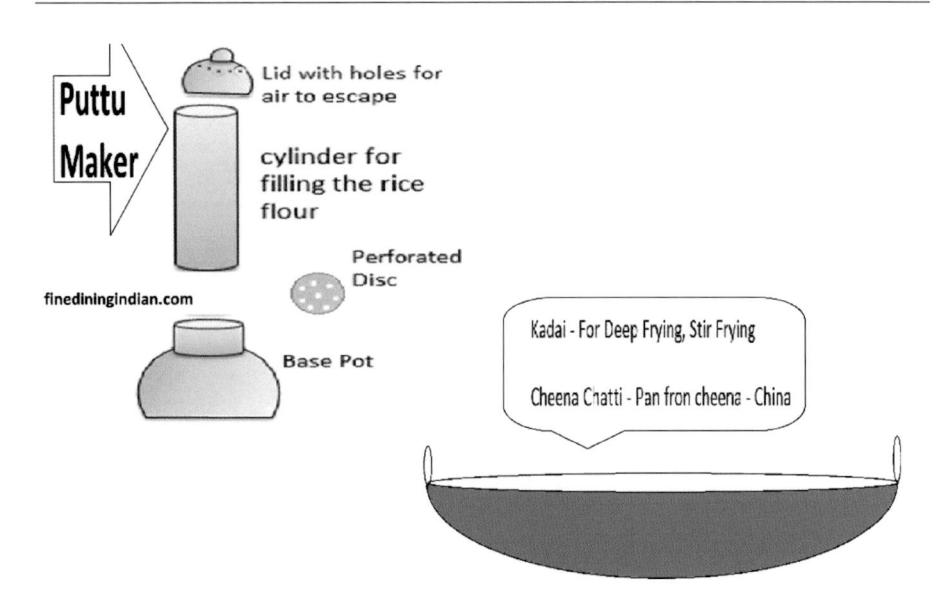

Beyond curry by bobby

Puttu Maker
- Lid with holes for air to escape
- cylinder for filling the rice flour
- Perforated Disc
- Base Pot

finediningindian.com

Kadai - For Deep Frying, Stir Frying

Cheena Chatti - Pan fron cheena - China

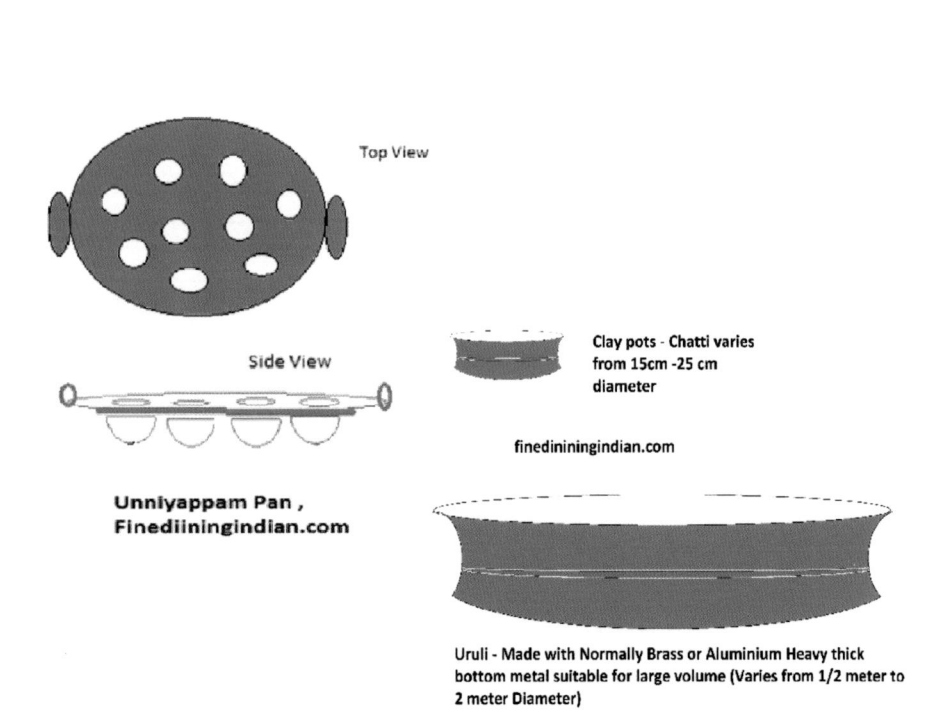

Top View

Side View

Unniyappam Pan, Finediiningindian.com

Clay pots - Chatti varies from 15cm -25 cm diameter

finedininingindian.com

Uruli - Made with Normally Brass or Aluminium Heavy thick bottom metal suitable for large volume (Varies from 1/2 meter to 2 meter Diameter)

Food Design Concepts

Food can stimulate several of our senses—sight, smell, taste, and touch. Food design can be explained as a selective and thoughtful process of cooking and presenting food to maximize its visual appeal.

Food presentation is not limited to ready-to-eat foods; it starts from selecting the ingredients, the cooking process, the cuisine, the chef's skills, and the service wares. My perception of food will not be the same as yours, but visual appeal is mostly the same to everyone.

There is a great saying: "We eat with our eyes first." This is very true—an indifferently presented dish will not get any praise for the chef.

If, in reading this book, you gain wisdom about cooking and presenting an excellent dish, our vision will be achieved. Please pass the knowledge you gain on to your colleagues and juniors—"knowledge is to share, and to share is to care."

Food design is developed in a next-generation Indian cuisine movement by modifying, processing, arranging, or decorating food to enhance its aesthetic appeal.

Nouvelle cuisine chefs often consider the visual presentation of foods at many different stages of food preparation, from the manner of tying or sewing meats, to the type of cut used in chopping and slicing meats or vegetables, to the style of mould used in a baked dish.

The arrangement and overall styling of food on the plate is called "plating."

Some common styles of plating include a "classic" or "old school" arrangement in which the main item is in the front of the plate with vegetable or starches in the back, a "stacked" arrangement of the various items, or the main item leaning or "shingled" on a vegetable bed or side item.

Item location on the plate is often referenced as for the face of a clock, with six o' clock being the position closest to the diner.

A basic rule of plating, and even in some cases prepping, is to make sure you have the five components of a dish: protein, traditionally at a six o' clock position; vegetable, at a two o' clock position; starch, at an eleven o' clock position; sauce; and garnish.

This kind of plating is seen in culinary colleges only for teaching purposes.

Chefs are only limited by their own creativity when it comes to plate designs nowadays.

Clock styles are outdated, and many chefs don't follow guidelines. Instead, they use an abstract style, line style, pattern style, or even serve food straight on the cooking pan.

Lateral Arrangement

Slow roast lamb loin, coconut tossed rice dumpling, str-fried spinach. In this style, we tried to arrange food on a line with alternate textures and items and focused on texture and cooking, since it is a medium rare lamb loin. This style is fit for a confident chef to show off his or her meat-cooking skills.

Beyond curry by bobby

Stacked Style

Fennel spiced pan-roasted wood pigeon, In this style, ingredients stacked together and give focus to natural food color's.

Factors in Food Design

How, what, where

These factors have to complement each other. When combined, they will result in excellent food presentation. You have learned two presentation styles and how to maximize your cooking skills and ingredients used. Sometimes you need to play with contrasting colors when presenting complex dishes (more than three main ingredients)

We learned cooking is the art and science of good eating. In addition, it can be defined as the study of food and culture, with a particular focus on gourmet cuisine. In Indian cuisine, the cultural influence on food is very high, and as Indians, we have to preserve our cultural heritage.

How

This factor defines the material in which you are going to serve the food. It can be any kind of material, such as metal, ceramic, or wood. However, make sure it does not react with the food ingredients. Plates can come in any shape or size. You should carefully select appropriate plates. The food placed in the plate should get 100 per cent of the attention, so the plate you select should act as a canvas for your food.

For dark-colored food items, try to choose white plates.For light-colored food items, you can try colored or shaded plates. For saucy dishes, try deep plates with larger rims.Keep one thing in mind: whatever the plate is, it has to be large enough to leave empty space. We strongly suggest you try the same food on different plates to find the best one.

What

The food you place on the plate should get the prime focus, and your plate will support you to get the result.When you plan your food, it should be balanced in color, texture, and flavor. These three factors in food are the first we experience through our senses. They have a big impact on presenting the food.

Color

The color of the food is the first element that influences our senses. You can include colors by using natural ingredients alone or combining them, including spinach, tomato, turmeric, milk, and squid ink.Would you hesitate to eat an orange that was purple in color? You would probably be reluctant.

People associate certain colors with certain flavors, and the color of food can influence the perceived flavor in anything from candy to wine. "Natural" foods such as oranges and salmon are sometimes also dyed to mask natural variations in color. Color variation in foods throughout the seasons and the effects of processing and storage often make color addition commercially advantageous to maintain the color expected or preferred by the consumer.

Texture

Texture is the combined effect of physical variation from liquid, soft, hard, or brittle states. Texture/body/mouthfeel is a product's physical and chemical interaction in the mouth, an aspect of food rheology. Texture is a concept used in many areas related to the testing and valuating of foodstuffs, and it is evaluated from initial perception on the palate, to first bite, through mastication to swallowing and aftertaste. Many people will relate texture to a product's water content, hard or crisp products having lower water content and soft products having intermediate to high water content. You always have the liberty to provide external textures to your dish, if it lacks texture combinations.

For example, you can use tuile, parmesan crisp, vegetable crisp, or freeze-dried fruits. In Indian cuisine, we have an amazing range of dishes that vary in texture. In savoury, we have pappadums, kasta rotis, bujias, and more to give a crunchy texture to our meal.

Flavor

Flavor, or aroma, is the factor that makes us feel the food is appetizing. If we preserve the flavor until it gets to the table, we are successful. In Indian cuisine, we have numerous spices that can influence flavor in a food. Use them wisely; some flavors can stop us from eating the food, whereas some can tempt us into having more. Your personal liking of flavors will not be the same as your guests', so keep a common flavor balance. If you are trying something new, ask for the opinions of your colleagues and regular guests before putting the dish on the menu.

Flavor is the sensory impression of a food or other substance, and it is determined mainly by the chemical senses of taste and smell. The flavor of the food can be altered with natural or artificial flavorings, which affect these senses.

Flavoring is defined as a substance that gives another substance flavor, altering its characteristics and causing it to become sweet, sour, tangy, and so on. The perfect seasoning also enhances the flavor tremendously. In Chinese cuisine, they season almost all dishes with salt and sugar, which results in bringing up the flavors that stimulate our appetite.

Of the three chemical senses, smell is the main determinant of flavor. While the taste of food is limited to sweet, sour, bitter, salty, and savoury (umami)—the basic tastes—the smells of a food are potentially limitless. A food's flavor, therefore, can be easily altered by changing its smell while keeping its taste similar.

Nowhere is this better exemplified than in artificially flavored jellies, soft drinks, and candies, which, while made of bases with a similar taste, have dramatically different flavors due to the use of different scents or fragrances.

Taste

Taste is one of the five traditional senses and is received through taste buds situated in the mouth and tongue. Taste is perceived as sweet, bitter, sour, salty, and umami.

Umami

This taste makes you feel like licking your finger after a tasty meal. If we identify those mixtures, we can replicate the delicious umami effect in each of our dishes. In Indian food, knowingly or unknowingly, we use lot of umami-rich ingredients.

One kind of taste enhancer, "chat masala," has a similar effect. That is why our traditional tandoor chefs dust every kebab with chat masala—it makes you want more. Tomato is one of the natural fruits enriched with high umami content, and we use tomatoes in high quantities.

Where

This is the most important factor that will determine how your food is perceived.

You might have come up with a fantastic presentation, excellent food, and a great plate, but all of this will be worthless if you serve the food in a multicolored discotheque or dimly lit pub.

Therefore, this factor is very important even though we're talking about this last. Food presentation is a cyclic process that is dependent on each factor.

If you overlook one factor, then the purpose is not served. However, you can always re-evaluate the process before you finalize your dishes.

We strongly suggest that when you do plating, food trials, or tasting, you taste the food as a guest would even if you pay for the cost. That will allow you to understand the value you will get as a guest.

Some points we can consider about the where factor:

- Color and lighting of the place
- Tablecloth
- Outdoor or indoor
- Theme of the service
- Time of service

Starting Your Own Restaurant

Working for yourself is a great and bold decision—stick to it.

I suggest it is better to have a service industry background to start a restaurant business. If you are only a promoter, it's fine when you have an expert team to take care of your business.

You need to have a strong plan and make several decisions before you take your first step.

Once you have made your decision, never look back, whatever hardship it may take to make your plan a reality.

"Any remarkable journey starts with a single step."

Beyond curry by bobby

Style of Restaurant Service

You should decide the type of service according to the clientele you wish to cater to. Clientele can be varied according to your restaurant's location.

A city centre restaurant in a commercial hub can be best suited for fast-paced, informal dining service.

A site close to a residential area with a wealthy clientele crowd around can be a good place for a formal fine dining restaurant.

Casual Dining

In casual dining, the service is maintained at the required level to meet the customer's expectations.

Most casual dining operates with a lower staff-to-guest ratio. In this service style, you do not need to maintain a high level of service standards.

You can run a casual dining service with employees of minimal service industry experience. However, train the team in the service you want to deliver.

Fine Dining

In the fine dining style of service, the guest is offered the full service option. Staff members are required to be well trained and highly professional in attitude.

The fine dining service style is costly in day-to-day operation. However, you can demand the price for the service and food you provide with confidence.

Beyond curry by bobby

In India, stand-alone fine dining restaurants are less common compared to other similar European metropolitan areas. The reason is the cost involved and high standards to maintain. However, many five-star hotels have at least one fine dining restaurant, and most of them serve Indian cuisine.

When you want to provide fine dining service and food, everything you select for your restaurant should be of high quality, from the color of the paint used in your restaurant to the staff uniform, and from the plates used to the meat selection in the menu.

Hard work and dedicated passion to excellent food are required to maintain the stature of the restaurant at the top level.

For fine dining food presentation and cooking methods, chefs give extra care that adds to the value.

Fine dining restaurants provide a memorable experience of service and food.

There are many unwritten rules of fine dining restaurants, including concept-based menus, amuse-bouche before any orders, and tasting or degustation menu options.

Chefs come up with their own ideology to be competitive enough in today's fast-paced culinary revolution.

Pre-Opening Stage

Once you have decided which style you'd like adapt, start planning backwards from your ideal opening date.

All your strategies and ideas can be put down in black and white; this will help later when you're stuck somewhere. The first thing you need to prepare is a detailed business plan.

A business plan can be explained as a detailed list of steps that are required for starting up and smoothly running any business.

People often think a business plan is only essential for start-ups to secure financial assistance. This is incorrect; since a business plan is a detailed version of a business's vision and strategies, it will always be relevant.

A good business plan must contain detailed background information about the business, the operational plan, the marketing plan, the financial plan, decision-making criteria, and so on.

Based on your business plan, create a checklist that contains the task, the person responsible, the time frame, and the status of task. The checklist is very essential in tracking your business development.

An ideal task list can include naming the restaurant, developing a vision and mission statement, finding a location for the restaurant, identifying and applying for the licences required, pre-opening marketing plans, advertising for job vacancies, recruiting, training, and procurement of hard and soft items.

A large and detailed list ensures that all areas are covered and that you can peacefully work through the list without being distracted by other opinions.

Recruiting the right staff with the right attitude is the key part in the pre-opening stage. Your staff has to believe in your restaurant's vision.

When all your hard work is in place and the opening day comes, give your best service, which the customers may not expect from day one.

Keep an eye on competition and market trends, and always cater to your loyal customers' expectations.

Create your own marketing strategies by involving local community and charity organizations and organizing events for them.

Remember that word of mouth is always the best, cheapest, and most long-term advertisement method—use it wisely.

Best wishes for your venture. I will be privileged to help you.

Beyond curry by bobby

The Recipe Collection

"Whatever meat you cook, respect the ingredients; a life is lost in the transition to being a food commodity."

Poultry Recipes

The most common in poultry is chicken, but I prefer locally grown country chicken, which takes long hours to cook.
Other food source birds found in Kerala houses are duck, quail, turkey, pigeon, and occasionally wild birds, although these are illegal.

Beyond curry by bobby

*T*raditional country chicken   **63**

*T*oddy shop–inspired chicken delicacy   **67**

*W*ood pigeon with coconut   **71**

*C*hicken and vegetable stew   **74**

*D*uck roasted and braised   **77**

Traditional Country chicken curry,

Steamed savory rice pudding (Idli) tossed in gunpowder. (Nadan kozhi curry)

Serves: 2
Course: starter

For chicken wings

4 country chicken wings
40 mL coconut oil
2 g mustard seed
1 whole red chili
4 curry leaves
3 g chopped ginger
4 g chopped garlic

50 g chopped onion
3 g turmeric powder
5 g coriander powder
5 g red chili powder
50 g chopped tomato
50 mL coconut milk
Salt to taste

For spice fried idli

1 idli **(page 142)**
20 mL clarified butter
5 g gunpowder **(page 161)**
Salt to taste

Clean and trim chicken wings, keeping the skin intact for flavor.

Heat oil and add mustard seeds and red chili; allow mustard to crackle. By then, the red chili must have turned dark brown; remove and discard. The chili is used for infusing the flavor.

Sautéing continuously, immediately add ginger, then garlic. When this turns golden, add onion; sauté until light brown.

Now add the chicken pieces, and sprinkle salt in the sauce until the skin gets caramel-colored. Salt helps in getting color quickly by removing water from the skin.

When the chicken is colored, add all powdered spices and sauté for 30 seconds. If the pan is hot, sauté by removing from direct fire; this helps prevent the spices from being burned.

Add chopped tomato and allow it cook for a minute. Add water just to get enough sauce to cover the chicken wings.

Allow to cook over medium heat; check frequently to ensure you get enough liquid.
Once the chicken is cooked, finish with coconut milk; check and adjust seasoning.

For spice fried idli

Dice idli into 10 equal cubes as shown in the picture; each plate gets 5. Heat a flat pan and sauté idli pieces in clarified butter.

Once the golden color is achieved, sprinkle with gunpowder and salt. Keep in a kitchen towel in a warm place.

For plating

Consider using a deep pasta plate. Place the wings with a spoon of sauce in the centre; arrange idli pieces around, keeping equal distances between chicken and idli; spoon on the sauce; and garnish with micro herbs. We used mustard flower as it goes with the flavor.

Suggestions:

For restaurants, this is a brilliant idea of utilizing one dish for garnish and as a bread side portion. For home, this is a recycling idea for extra idlis that were cooked for breakfast.

Try the chicken curry recipe with other chicken parts, boneless pieces if it's a restaurant. Then it's best to add some chicken stock for more flavor and body for the curry sauce.

Toddy shop-inspired fried chicken delicacy
With pickled shallots, chili-toasted dosa pancake
(karal varuthathu)

Serves: 2
Course: starter

100 g chicken liver
100 g chicken hearts
100 g chicken gizzard
(all of the above called offals)

Beyond curry by bobby

First marinade

10 g fennel powder
15 g ginger garlic paste
5 g pepper powder
10 g chili powder
5 mL lime juice
Salt to taste

Second marinade

20 g coconut powder
10 g rice flour

Dosa crisp

10 g ghee
4 dosa pancakes **(page 142)**

To finish

200 mL coconut oil
4 pickled shallots*
2 g micro cress

Soak offals in cold milk overnight. Before preparation, remove from milk and remove any fat bits or fibres around the meat. Wash thoroughly and pat dry.

Marinate chicken offals with first marinade ingredients and salt as required. Mix with second marinade and set aside.

Trim dosa pancake to a slab of 4 cm by 7 cm. Toast in a pan by smearing ghee until golden in color. Sprinkle with chili powder and salt.

Shallow-fry the marinated offals using coconut oil, just enough to give a good crispy outside but pink inside to keep the natural flavor of delicate offals.

Remove and keep in paper towels to rest. Slice the pieces, arrange on top of toasted dosa, and place sliced pickled onion and micro cress on top.

Suggestions:

When frying, try not to crowd the pan; allow to color before you turn the sides.

Resting is as important as your cooking. If you try to cut the offals early, the juices will be lost and result in a dry meat texture.

The spice level can be increased by adding or reducing the chili powder quantity.

*Pickled shallots you may buy from the market, or preserve in a pickling mixture—1 part water, 4 parts neutral vinegar, whole spices, 0.5 part salt, 0.5 part sugar.

Warm all together, cool down, and pour in jar with peeled shallots. Use after 48 hours.

Toddy shops are great culinary retreats where spiced, aromatic dishes are made to accompany the purest toddy that is obtained by naturally fermented sap from the coconut tree.

Stir-fried wood pigeon with coconut

(Pravu thoran) a Kerala style stir-fry preparation with grated coconut.

Serves: 4
Course: main

720 g wood pigeon

First stage
30 mL coconut oil
10 g ginger-garlic paste
3 g turmeric powder
50 g shallots, sliced

10 g red chili powder
2 sliced chilies
1 sprig curry leaf
500 mL chicken stock or water
Salt to taste

Second stage
For stir-frying

50 mL coconut oil
3 g mustard seeds
1 sprig curry leaf
10 g chopped ginger
2 green chilies, sliced lengthwise
100 g shallots, peeled
3 g turmeric powder
5 g crushed fennel seed
10 g coriander powder
10 g jeera powder
50 g fresh grated coconut
Salt to taste

Joint wood pigeon to 30–40 g pieces with bone . For fine cooking, de-bone and make stock with bones.

Mix pigeon pieces with ingredients mentioned in first stage except oil and stock.

Heat a thick-bottomed pan with oil and add the pigeon mix. Sauté to sear evenly, add stock, and cook the meat until tender.

Reduce the stock and allow the stock to absorb completely into the meat.

For the second stage, heat coconut oil in a stir-fry pan, and splutter mustard seeds, curry leaf, ginger-garlic paste, and green chili. Sauté lightly and add peeled shallots.

Mix in all powdered spices, crushed fennel seeds, and cooked pigeon pieces. Stir-fry until all the spices are mixed properly, and it starts giving a roast flavor. Check seasoning and finish with fresh grated coconut.

Sauté for a few seconds until the coconut is spread evenly. Serve in a deep plate garnished with micro cress, or arrange on a flat plate.

Suggestion:

Game birds require long cooking periods. You can adapt modern cooking techniques of sous vide, which help in controlled slow cooking.

Beyond curry by bobby

Corn-fed chicken and vegetable stew
Stews are inherited from the colonial period stew. (Istew)

Vegetable stew presented with chapatti (whole-wheat bread) in stacked up style

Serves: 2
Course: main

2 corn-fed chickens supreme

For chicken
3 g turmeric
2 g cardamom powder
3 g garlic paste
3 g pepper powder
Salt to taste

For vegetable stew
100 g peeled, diced carrot
100 g peeled, diced potato
50 g peas, peeled
5 cardamom pods
2 bay leaves
100 g diced onion
4 slit green chilies
20 g chopped ginger
200 g coconut milk powder
Salt to taste
30 mL coconut oil
2 g mustard seed
1 sprig curry leaf

Marinate chicken supreme with ingredients mentioned in marinade. Cover and refrigerate. Boil 400 ml water with cardamom, bay leaf, ginger, and green chilies; add potato when half-done, then add carrot and onion. When both are cooked, add peeled fresh peas. Remove from fire and strain and discard cardamom, green chilies, and bay leaf. In remaining stock, dilute coconut milk powder

Heat coconut oil in a saucepan. Add mustard seed and allow to crackle, then add curry leaf and strained vegetables. Pour in coconut milk, simmer for a minute, check seasoning, and keep out from fire.

Pan-fry chicken breast skin side first to a light brown color, then fry the other side. Finish in oven, rest for 2 minutes, and serve on top of hot vegetable stew.

Suggestions:

Vegetables should not be overcooked, and the color should be preserved. You can finish with a pinch of cardamom powder.

Slow roasted and braised duck fillet,
Potato cooked in Spiced coconut sauce.
(Tharavu mappas)

In this recipe, you can make traditional duck (tharavu) mappas, which is done in a curry style, and combine with a slow-roasted duck breast with greater control in cooking texture.

Serves: 2
Course: main

Slow-roasted duck
2 duck breasts
10 mL lime juice
10 g ginger garlic paste
3 g turmeric powder
10 g coriander powder
7 g chili powder

For duck mappas
2 duck breasts, diced
300 mL duck stock or water
1 g cloves
1 bay leaf
2 g cinnamon
50 mL coconut oil
2 g mustard seeds
1 sprig curry leaves
100 g white onion, sliced
10 g ginger garlic paste
2 green chilies, sliced

3 g turmeric powder
7 g chili powder
10 g coriander powder
5 g fennel powder
5 g garam masala powder
70 g tomato, diced
150 g coconut milk powder
100 g potato (1-cm cubes)
Salt to taste

Trim duck breast, removing excess skin or fat. Dice one breast into cubes, same as potato; for the second one, score on skin side (ideal for pan roasting). Marinate both duck breasts separately with a pinch of turmeric, chili, salt, and 2 g ginger garlic paste.

Boil diced duck meat very tender with duck stock, clove, bay leaf, cinnamon, and a few sliced onions. When the duck is soft, pick out and discard the whole spices. Dilute coconut milk powder by adding stock and keeping a thick consistency.

Heat oil in a thick-bottomed pan, add mustard seed, and let crackle. Add sliced onion and ginger garlic paste; sauté until light brown. Add all spice powders and sauté on slow heat without burning.

Mix in tomato and cooked duck along with the stock. Bring to a boil and simmer. Stir in coconut milk, add potato cubes, and cook slowly without bubbling until potato is cooked.

Meanwhile, pan sear the second duck breast skin side first, apply coconut oil, and turn until the skin is nicely browned.

Roast in a preheated oven at 180 °C until the core temperature of the meat reaches 63 °C or even less as per your taste. Allow it to rest for half of your cooking time before slicing; this will help all juices get reabsorbed by the meat tissue. For the sauce, check seasoning and adjust consistency as per your requirements; ideally, it should have a thick, creamy texture.

Spoon stewed duck onto two deep plates and trim sides of roasted breast. Divide in two equal pieces and place on centre; garnish with micro cress.

Suggestions:
Duck should be treated the same as red meat and given enough time to rest after roasting. It's best to cook it medium rare.

Seafood Recipes

Kerala being coastal area seafood is great source for food. We get the best prawns, crab and sea water fishes. Few selected recipes are given here, many recipes can be substituted with fish or seafood available near you.

Beyond curry by bobby

Seafood

www.finediningindian.com

Steamed and seared haddock loin **83**

Kerala spice king prawn **87**

Pan fried rainbow trout **90**

Banana leaf wrapped pearl spot **93**

Salmon in coconut sauce **95**

Sauted crab **98**

Steamed and seared haddock loin,

gingered vegetables, curried cauliflower emulsion, cardamom, and lime air. (**meen vevicathu**)

Serves: 2
Course: main

For fish

340 g haddock fillet
5 g garlic puree

2 g turmeric powder
2 g green chili paste
10 mL oil
Salt to taste

For cardamom and lime air
10 g cardamom powder
10 mL lime juice
5 g lecithin powder
100 mL thin coconut milk
For vegetables
70 g fine beans
30 g carrot
20 g peeled peas
2 g cumin seed
10 mL oil
1 g pepper
Salt to taste

For cauliflower emulsion
100 g cauliflower florets
20 g butter
2 g turmeric powder
20 g chopped shallots
30 mL thick coconut milk
30 mL water
1 g white pepper powder
Salt to taste

Cut fish to equally sized portions; marinate with mentioned ingredients for fish and set aside.

Blanch fine beans, cut in equal lengths, and split in half. Dice carrot to 0.5-cm cubes and blanch.

Heat a thick-bottomed saucepan with butter, shallots, and turmeric; sauté for 30 seconds.

Add sliced cauliflower and sauté for a minute; pour in water and coconut milk, and cook slowly until the cauliflower is tender. Check seasoning. Puree to a very fine emulsion using a commercial blender.

In a deep mixing bowl, mix lecithin powder, cardamom powder, and warm, thin coconut milk. Blend using a hand blender; stop when the foam starts coming up.

Add lime juice; during plating, blend again until you get strong foam that stands when you take it in a spoon.

Heat oil in a small frying pan; add cumin seed and toss in all the vegetables you prepared before. Season and place on a kitchen paper to remove excess oil.

When time to serve, steam fish in a steamer or steamer basket, placing skin side on top.

Remove the fish when it's 80 per cent done. Pan-fry the skin side using a non-stick pan or greaseproof paper.

Start plating the vegetables as per the picture; when the fish gets golden in color, place on top of the beans with skin side on top.

Heat and spoon the cauliflower emulsion as shown in the picture, and place a spoonful of cardamom air on top of fish.

Suggestions:

For steaming, consider using flat fish or flat cuts of fish, which helps in cooking evenly.

Pan searing the skin after steaming provides a unique crispy texture to steamed fish.

Kerala spice coated crispy king prawn
(chemmen varuthathu)

Same recipe can be tried with anchovies

www.finediningindian.com

Serves: 1
Course: starter

3 king prawns
1 g turmeric powder
3 mL lime juice
2 garlic cloves
4 curry leaves
1 g black peppercorn
5 g shallot, peeled
5 g dry shrimp powder
2 g red chili powder
2 g coriander powder
3 g coconut milk powder
1 no: mini poppadum
200 mL oil
Salt to taste

For beetroot air
Follow the same method as for cardamom lime air in meen vevichathu; add beetroot juice plus all other ingredients.

Remove shell from king prawns, leaving the head and tail, devein, and marinate with salt, lime juice, and turmeric. Coarsely grind garlic, shallots, pepper, and curry leaf, and mix in with prawns; keep for 10 minutes.

Now add and mix all dry powder. Check salt and leave in fridge for 10 minutes before frying; this is to avoid losing spices when the prawns are dropped in hot oil.

Heat oil to 160 °C, as this is best for frying without burning the spices yet gives a crisp texture. After frying prawn strain the oil fry mini poppadum in same and discard the oil , it may not advisable to re-use oil after second tme.

Suggestions:

You can try the same recipe with fresh, cleaned calamari (squid) rings, anchovy, white bait.. Quickly fry it without overcooking to keep it soft, but with a crisp spice coating.

If you need a more crispy texture, add Japanese bread crumbs (the crumbs have more similarity to desiccated coconut). Large crumbs give the right mouthfeel.

Beyond curry by bobby

Pan fried spicy rainbow trout
(meen porichathu)

Serves: 4
Course: main

4 fillets rainbow trout
4 baby plums
2 sprigs coriander leaf

First marinade

2 g turmeric powder
Salt to taste
Juice of 1 lemon

Second marinade

1 sprig curry leaf
5 garlic cloves
10 g fennel seeds
5 shallots
10 g black peppercorn
5 g red chili powder
10 g coriander powder

Clean the fish, check for any bones, wash, and pat dry. Score fish on skin side, apply first marinade, and set aside.

Grind together curry leaf, fennel seeds, peppercorn, shallots, and garlic to a smooth paste; mix in coriander powder, chili powder, and salt; and apply the mixture evenly on both sides of the fish.

Keep refrigerated for at least half an hour. Heat coconut oil in a thick-bottomed pan. Fry fish on skin side until 80 per cent done on medium, turn, and remove to a kitchen towel.

The fish will cook fast depending on thickness; keep it moist for a brilliant mouthfeel. Pan-fry plum tomatoes; serve with coriander leaf.

Suggestions:

Oily fish is best suited for pan-frying, including mackerel, trout, salmon, and sardine.

For restaurants, you can keep the marinade ready in advance; apply the first marinade, then the second, and cook when ready to serve.

Lobster, prawn, fresh clam, and mussel can be pan-fried using this style of marinade.

Banana leaf wrapped pearl spot
(Karimeen pollichathu)

A traditional Kerala preparation where fish is spiced, wrapped in banana leaf, and cooked on a hot iron griddle. Karimeen is the local name for pearl spot, which is a freshwater fish native to Kerala backwaters.

Serves: 4
Course: main

4 pearl spot, cleaned
100 mL coconut oil
1 tender banana leaf

For marinade
10 shallots
100 g onions
10 g ginger
20 g garlic
15 g chili powder
5 g pepper powder
10 mL vinegar
1 sprig curry leaves
Salt to taste

Make a rough paste with all the ingredients mentioned. Score the fish on sides; apply the marinade on both sides.

Place the fish in the banana leaf and wrap gently.

Apply oil on a hot griddle. Gently place the wrapped fish in the griddle, cover with a lid, and cook on a low fire until both sides are done.

Suggestions:

Try with fillet of flat fish, such as turbot, sole, or John Dory. you have the option of serving fish in banana leaf or remove and present in your own style

Slow braised salmon in turmeric spiked coconut milk (meen molly)

A light fish preparation with coconut milk that is braised slowly, flavored with turmeric, and spiced with pepper and green chili; best served with appam.

Serves: 4
Course: main

600 g salmon
3 g turmeric
5 g salt

For molly sauce

50 mL coconut oil
2 g fenugreek seed
5 g mustard
1 g sprig curry leaves
20 g garlic, thinly sliced
30 g ginger, thinly sliced
150 g onion, sliced
4 green chilies, chopped
15 g turmeric
200 g coconut milk powder
5 baby plum tomatoes
Salt to taste
150 mL water or plain fish stock

Portion the fish into 50 g pieces, marinate with turmeric and salt, pan-fry with coconut oil to sear evenly, and set aside.

Dilute coconut milk powder to get a thick consistency. Heat coconut oil in a deep, thick-bottomed saucepan, add mustard seeds, and allow to crackle.

Add curry leaf, ginger, and garlic, and sauté to light golden; then add sliced onion, and sauté for a minute.

Add chopped green chili; sauté to remove the raw chili flavor. Add turmeric powder and salt, and sauté without sticking to the pan. Pour in water or fish stock; reduce heat to a simmer.

Now add thick coconut milk, adjust seasoning, and slide in the fish pieces. Avoid stirring; rather, try moving pieces by moving the pan.

Add halved baby plum tomatoes; simmer for 15 minutes over low heat without boiling.

Results are better when consumed after an hour, when flavors are settled properly.

Suggestions:
Choose firm, fresh, oily fish, preferably round fish. After adding coconut milk, do not boil; adjust spiciness using crushed black pepper.

Crab sautéed with kerala spices
(Njandu piralan)

An old-fashioned Kerala crab (njandu) preparation originating from coastal areas, cooked in its own shells and sautéed with spices.

Serves: 2
Course: main

400 g crab
30 mL coconut oil
5 g chopped ginger
5 g garlic, chopped
100 g shallots, sliced
1 sprig curry leaves
3 g turmeric powder
10 g chili powder
10 g coriander powder
8 g tamarind paste
2.5 g fenugreek powder
Salt to taste

Wash the crab well. Ensure that all dirt from the shell is removed. Wash it with a bristle scrubber if required.

Remove legs and claws, break each into two, and lightly crack the bigger pieces—this will help the spices get to the meat easily.

Remove the top shell from main body and discard. Clean the meat that is in the bottom shell.

Clear all hairy, hard, and spongy textures from the shell. Cut into four pieces.

For making njandu piralan:

Heat oil on medium high heat in a pan, add curry leaves and stir. Add ginger and garlic, and sauté; when it is light brown, add sliced onion and sauté until golden.

Reduce heat to medium, add chili powder, coriander powder, turmeric powder, and fenugreek powder, and roast well.

Add the tamarind mixture and mix well. Raise heat to medium high, add the water, and bring to a boil.

Add salt and mix well. Add the crab pieces and mix well. Cook covered, mixing occasionally.

Cook for about 15 minutes, remove cover, and cook until the gravy is thick enough to coat the crab.

Suggestions:

For best results, cook at night, reheat, and reduce the gravy the next day. Do not refrigerate during the night. This way, the meat will absorb the spices well. Lobsters are a best option for this method of cooking.

In Kerala when we cook crab or shellfish we don't pre-cook to remove the meat of kill the shellfish before cooking.

Red Meat Recipes

In Kerala after chicken, beef is most cooked meat, and then comes lamb. Even though there are Hindus people in Kerala are very fond of beef. Mostly the beef termed for the meat taken from buffalo as cow slaughtering considered sin as per Hindu belief.

Beyond curry by bobby

*S*low braised lamb   103

*L*amb liver pepper roast   107

*S*tewed and stir-fried beef 111

Tender lamb Slow braised in spicy coconut broth, Carrot cumin puree, appam, fried egg yolk, and caramelized vegetables. (aatirachi curry)

The plate is a dedication to Christian and Muslim communities for their contributions to Kerala culinary history. Lamb masala is inspired by the Muslim preparation of Malabar region, and the egg appam is from the Christian household.

Serves: 4
Course: main

For lamb masala
600 g lamb breast, diced
30 mL coconut oil
5 g mustard seeds

1 sprig curry leaf
15 g ginger, thin sliced
20 g garlic, thin sliced
2 green chilies, sliced
150 g onions, chopped
5 g turmeric powder
10 g coriander powder
10 g cumin powder
15 g chili powder
5 g garam masala powder
700 mL mutton stock
Salt to taste

For carrot puree
100 g carrot
20 g grated coconut
3 g cumin
5 mL oil

For slow-dried vegetables
12 carrot ribbons, sliced fine
8 onions, sliced fine
100 g sugar
100 g water
For plating
2 appam (page 145)
12 sprigs mint cress
4 eggs

Marinate diced lamb with one-third of turmeric, chili powder, ginger, garlic, and green chilies. Add salt and boil, adding lamb stock over slow heat until tender and soft; this may take up to an hour and a half.

Meanwhile, make carrot puree by lightly sautéing carrot with cumin and coconut in hot oil and pureeing finely.
For dried vegetables, make stock syrup with boiling sugar and water until you get one stringy consistency.

Dip sliced vegetables in syrup, arrange on greaseproof paper or silicon mat, and dry in a pre-heated oven with a temperature of 85 °C for 2 hours. Keep in oven for longer if the texture is not crisp enough.

Heat coconut oil, and add mustard seeds, curry leaf, ginger, garlic, and green chili slices; sauté until light in color. Add onion and sauté until light brown, then add all remaining spice powder and sauté, keeping the pan away from direct fire.

Add cooked lamb pieces, mix well, and put back in fire. Sauté again without burning the spices. Add lamb stock, bring to a boil, and allow to simmer gently. Dilute coconut milk powder to a thick, creamy consistency by adding warm water.

When the sauce reaches a thick consistency, mix in the coconut milk and stir until you get a shiny, smooth finished lamb sauce. Keep on a warm surface ready for plating.

For plating, cut appam into four equal rectangular slabs. Fry eggs and cut yolks using a round cutter. Arrange lamb masala on top of appam slab, place fried egg and vegetable crisp as shown in picture, spoon on drops of carrot puree, and finish with mint cress.

Suggestions:

The method can be used for cooking game meats. Eggs can be substituted with quail eggs, which have more nutrients than normal eggs.

Lamb liver pepper roast

Combined with beetroot pachadi, broken wheat, and vegetable upma. (aatin karal kurumilagittathu)

Serves: 4
Course: main

For lamb liver fry
400 g lamb liver
200 mL milk
5 g ginger garlic paste
2 g turmeric powder
5 g fennel powder
10 g chili powder
100 mL oil

For pepper roast masala

50 mL coconut oil
5 g mustard seeds
4 green chilies
5 g ginger garlic paste
4 shallot halves
1 sprig curry leaves
100 g onion, sliced
4 g turmeric powder
5 g fennel powder
10 g coriander powder
5 g chili powder
5 g black pepper powder
50 g sliced tomato
Salt to taste

For wheat upma

20 mL oil
2 g mustard seeds
60 g broken wheat, dry
30 g courgette brunoise
30 g carrot brunoise
30 g onion brunoise
Salt to taste

For beetroot pachadi
Please refer to page 129

Slice lamb liver to a thickness of 1–2 cm, cover, and soak in milk for 2 hours (refrigerated).

Clean thoroughly, wash, and pat dry. Marinate liver with ingredients mentioned, except oil; cover and refrigerate.

For pepper roast masala, heat coconut oil in a thick-bottomed pan, add mustard seeds and allow to crack, then add each fresh ingredient in the order listed.

Sauté in between until the raw smell fades. Now add all remaining powder spices and salt; sauté without burning.

Add tomato, sauté, and check seasoning. Add stock or water to give a shiny moist finish to the masala.

For wheat upma, wash, boil, and strain broken wheat. Sauté with oil, mustard, and vegetables mentioned.

Pan-fry marinated lamb liver to medium or medium-rare (pink inside, yet crispy outside); trim sides to show the cooking.

Spread warm vegetable upma, spoon on pepper masala mix, and place sliced lamb liver on top.

Line with beetroot pachadi and finish with micro cress.

Suggestions:

Use only good quality lamb liver, which is dark red and has no other smell than fresh meat. Soaking in milk is very important to clear all impurities.

Stewed and stir-fried beef with coconut slices (Maatirachi ularthiyathu)

Often in Kerala, we use buffalo meat. Here we adapt two cooking styles—stewing and then finishing the dish by stir-frying with coconut and crushed spices.

Serves: 4
Course: main

For beef marinade
500 g beef chunks
15 mL coconut oil
5 g turmeric powder
10 g coriander powder
15 g chili powder
50 g sliced onion
1 sprig curry leaf
Salt to taste

For spice mixture
7 g peppercorns
7 g fennel seeds
2 g cinnamon stick
2 g clove
2 g cardamom

For stir-frying
50 mL coconut oil
30 g thin coconut slices
2 sprigs curry leaves
4 green chilies
20 g garlic julienne
20 g ginger julienne
150 g shallots
15 g red chili flakes
Salt to taste

Dice beef into small cubes, wash, drain, and set aside.

Dry-roast the ingredients listed for spice mixture until spices give off their aroma and begin to get slightly darker; allow to cool. Grind spices into a coarse powder.

Marinate the beef pieces with half of above spice mix and all ingredients mentioned in beef marinade.

Sauté marinated beef in a thick-bottomed pan for a minute; add water or beef stock until the meat is covered and slow cook until the meat is tender.

If any liquid is left after the meat is tender, pick out the beef pieces, reduce the liquid by one-third, and mix in with beef pieces.

For stir-frying, heat a thick bottom sauté pan with coconut oil and add sliced coconut.

When it turns light golden, remove and keep on a kitchen paper.

In the same pan, add other ingredients mentioned for stir-frying one by one in the order listed while sautéing in between.

Now add cooked beef pieces and all remaining roasted powdered spices, and toss over medium-low fire for 5 minutes. Be careful not to burn the spices by overheating.

Once the beef starts to dry and has attained a dark brown color, add fried coconut slices and combine well.

Suggestions:

You can try this cooking style with alternate meats such as game (wild meat), pork, and venison.

For best results, make the first stage braised meat a day in advance, and preserve in the same liquid. Reheat and reduce the juice, then stir-fry next day. The flavor will be extraordinary.

Vegetable Recipes

Kerala has a great history for vegetarian cuisine right from the king's time. Once a king of Travancore wanted to have an innovative vegetarian dishes for his dinner, and the cook realized there was nothing left for king to try since he tried all recipes. he took all vegetable left overs and cooked them together with a secret coconut paste recipe. King loved it presented him the title of best cook.

Beyond curry by bobby

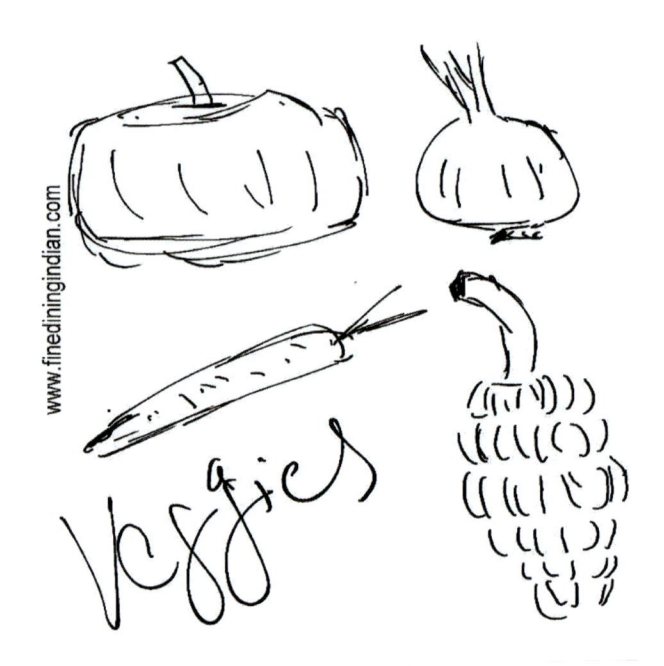

*M*élange of Kerala vegetables 117

*C*hickpeas in roasted coconut 120

*M*ushroom and shallots 123

*S*piced broth of Mixed vegetable and red lentil 125

*S*autéed Kerala spinach 128

*B*eetroot and yoghurt relish 129

*C*alicut street–style duck egg 130

Mélange of Kerala vegetables in coconut paste, (Avial)

A well-balanced mixed vegetable dish with cumin and curry leaf scented coconut paste, a must for all vegetarian feasts.

Serves: 4
Course: accompany main

Vegetables needed

150 g tender yam
150 g ash gourd
150 g raw banana
100 g beans
100 g carrots
100 g drumsticks
1 raw mango

For avial mix paste

100 g grated coconut
3 g cumin seeds
10 g ginger
3 green chilies
2 g turmeric powder
1 sprig curry leaves
Salt to taste
50 g yogurt

For finishing

1 sprig curry leaves
10 mL coconut oil

Wash, peel, and cut the vegetables to 5-cm length batons; marinate with turmeric and salt.

Cook, covered, in a flat-bottomed pan on slow fire until the vegetables are tender but have not lost color.

Meanwhile, grind the ingredients mentioned in avial paste together to a thick paste. If required, add just enough water to make a paste.

Now mix the paste with cooked vegetables. Cover and cook for 2 minutes; check seasoning.
To finish, warm coconut oil in a small pan. Add curry leaves and immediately pour over the cooked vegetables.

Suggestions:

Vegetables can be precooked beforehand by blanching in salted boiling water to keep the color. You can try any cuts or sizes to make the dish beautiful.

Chickpeas in roasted coconut sauce

(Kadala curry) "Kadala" is a local name for chickpea, a must combination for puttu

Serves: 4

Course: accompany main

100 g black/white chickpeas
30 mL coconut oil
2 g mustard seeds
60 g small onion chopped
10 g ginger garlic paste
1 sprig curry leaves
2 green chilies, slit in fours

30 g chopped tomato
1 g chopped coriander leaves
Salt to taste

For curry paste
60 g grated coconut
10 g coriander powder
5 g red chili powder
2 g turmeric powder
2 g fennel powder
2 g garam masala powder

Soak chickpeas until they split in one press, ideally overnight. Wash and strain chickpeas; cook starting with cold water just half an inch above the chickpea level, with salt to taste.

Cook until chickpeas are very tender and mash with one press; keep in low heat.

In a thick bottom frying pan, dry-roast grated coconut until it turns golden brown. Add all powdered spices mentioned for the curry paste; sauté until a pleasant flavor arises without burning.

Grind to a smooth paste, adding enough water; set aside.

Heat coconut oil in a deep pan; add mustard and allow to crack. When it begins to splutter, add sliced shallots, and sauté until light golden. Add ginger-garlic paste, sauté, then add curry leaves and green chilies.

Now add the ground curry paste and chopped tomato; mix slowly on medium heat.

Pour in cooked chickpeas along with water, and stir to mix well; check and adjust seasoning.

Simmer slowly until you get a well-balanced flavor; adjust the consistency by adding water if required.

Suggestions:

Chickpea curry may be used for any roast lamb dish garnish. For fine dining plating, play around with chickpeas, turning them into puree or crushed cake.

Mushrooms, shallots in coconut and tamarind sauce, (koonu ulli theeyal)

Serves: 2
Course: accompany main

100 g quartered button mushrooms
100 g sliced shallots
50 mL coconut oil
5 g mustard seed
10 g garlic thin strips
5 g chili powder
10 g coriander powder
1 sprig curry leaves
10 g tamarind pulp
5 g jaggery, diluted
Salt to taste

For theeyal paste

5 g cumin seeds
10 g peppercorn
15 g coriander seeds
2 red chilies (whole)
5 g fennel seed
100 g coconut, grated

Dry-roast all spices for theeyal paste, except coconut, until the aroma rises. Add grated coconut and sauté for giving a brown color and crispy texture.

Make a fine, smooth paste of grated, roasted coconut and spices by adding very little water.

In a saucepan, heat coconut oil; add mustard, curry leaf, and garlic; and sauté. Then add sliced shallots over medium heat until it becomes light brown.

Now add washed mushrooms and mix with powdered spices; sauté for a minute. Add theeyal paste to pan; sauté on low heat for 2 minutes. Add 100–150 mL water to get a sauce of semi-thick consistency.

Dilute jaggery in lukewarm water and add to sauce along with tamarind pulp; check seasoning. Simmer slowly until the mushroom is tender.

Suggestions:
The dish should be dark brown. If adding prawns, first remove dish from fire and add them while it's still hot. The prawns will be cooked to perfection. You can try it with prawns instead mushrooms.

Spiced broth of Mixed vegetable and red lentil (Sambar)

Classic mixed vegetarian dish similar to avial, a great combination with dosa/idli and rice.

Serves: 4
Course: accompany main

For lentils

50 g split yellow lentils (toor dal)
50 g red lentils (masoor dal)
2 g turmeric

For vegetables

50 g onion
50 g snake gourd
50 g carrot
50 g cluster beans
50 g okra
30 g colacasia /taro
30 g aubergine
100 g cucumber

1 drumstick
50 g potato
50 g tomato
50 g small onions

For flavoring

50 g sambar powder
50 mL tamarind juice
1 sprig coriander leaves

For tempering

50 mL coconut oil
1 g asafetida
5 g mustard seeds
3 dry red chilies
Curry leaves

Wash and boil lentils together with turmeric, salt, and four times as much water as lentils on medium heat, stirring in between. Wash, peel, and cut vegetables in 3-cm cubes, or whichever size you prefer.

When lentils are half done, add all vegetables to boiling lentil mix and allow the vegetables to cook, simmering slowly.

Now add ingredients for flavoring one by one, mixing in slowly without breaking vegetables. Simmer for a few minutes until the raw flavor of sambar spice disappears.

For tempering, heat a small pan and add ingredients mentioned one by one while sautéing in between. Pour immediately into the simmering sambar, cover with a lid, and remove from fire.

Allow the flavors to be infused. Check salt before serving. A properly seasoned sambar brings out very stimulating flavors.

Suggestions:

The color of the dish should be yellow to orange, with a melange of flavors arising when it's served. Asafetida should be used cautiously. Too much can turn the food bitter, but it's a great digestive supplement.

Sauted kerala spinach, mustard and curry leaf (Cheera mezukkupuratty)

Serves: 2
Course: accompany main

240 g baby green spinach / red spinach (cheera)
20 mL coconut oil
2 g mustard seeds
100 g shallots, chopped
10 g green chili, chopped
1 sprig curry leaves
Salt to taste

Wash, clean, and cut spinach. Shred or keep whole, but remove the stems. Heat oil in a pan. Splutter mustard seeds; then add chopped shallots and curry leaves, and sauté.
Finally, add spinach and salt. Keep covered and cook on low flame.

Suggestions:
The color should be dark brown. When you add fresh, cleaned prawn after removing from the fire, it turns into a perfect cooked prawn dish.

Beetroot and yoghurt relish,
mustard tempering, (Beetroot pachadi)

Serves: 2
Course: accompany main

150 g beetroots, diced
50 g coconut, grated
5 shallots, chopped
3 green chilies
5 g ginger, chopped
2 sprigs curry leaves
3 g mustard seeds
1 g fenugreek seeds
Salt to taste

Heat oil and add fenugreek seed. When it's light brown, add mustard seeds to crack. Add ginger, curry leaf, shallots, and green chilies; lightly sauté. Add beetroot and cook until soft, with enough water to cover the beetroot. When cooked, add grated coconut, grind to a fine puree, and adjust seasoning. Add curd according to desired thickness and taste. Use a hand blender to blend fine; if you desire a smooth finish, pass through a fine sieve. Pachadi can be served room temperature or warm.

Duck egg and sweet peas, Calicut streetstyle,
(Tharavu mutta pattani thoran)

Serves: 1
Course: starter/snack

2 duck eggs
15 mL coconut oil
1 g mustard seed
3 g chopped ginger
4 curry leaf
2 g chopped green chilly
20 g chopped onion
10 g grated coconut
10 g fresh peas
20 g chopped tomato
1 g white pepper powder
Salt to taste

Beat eggs in a small bowl with chopped onion, tomato, pepper, and salt. Heat coconut oil in a thick-bottomed, wok-style pan and add mustard seed.

When it starts cracking, add ginger and curry leaf; sauté for a minute.

Now add grated coconut; sauté until light golden in color. Add peas, sauté, and mix in beaten egg mix, stirring continuously without sticking. Check seasoning and serve hot.

Suggestion:

The egg should be bright and colorful with garnishes. This is a perfect dish for a lazy afternoon and is quick to make.

You can substitute with hen eggs, a good combination with tea or a light snack accompanied with bread. Any other form of edible egg would work as well. You may avoid coconut if it's not your taste and try with Japanese bread crumb instead.

Rice, Breads and other carbohydrates

Kerala produces most of the staples they consume. it of the largest collection of rice and breads preperations in india. Mostly consumed with curry or fried accompaniments. Few important kerala staple recipes are given here

Griddle cooked layered bread   134

Flaky bread tossed in chicken curry   139

Steamed savory rice pudding,

Dosa pan cake   142

Pancake with fermented rice batter   145

Sautéed and steamed rice flour cake   148

Spiced Lamb and basmati rice biryani   150

Boiled and sautéed Cassava,

Sea bass curry   155

Beyond curry by bobby

Griddle cooked layered porotta bread
(Kerala porotta)

Serves: 30–40
Course: accompany main

For dough

500 g plain flour
3 g baking powder
1 egg (medium hen)
4 g salt
6 g of sugar
240 mL milk
For cooking
150 mL neutral oil

In a mixing bowl, combine flour, baking powder, salt, and sugar, using a clean hand. Combine egg and flour mixture slowly.

Add milk little by little while combining the dough together; add plain water if required.

Knead tightly to get a tight dough, apply oil on surface, and cover with a moist cloth; rest for 30 minutes.

Beyond curry by bobby

For layers

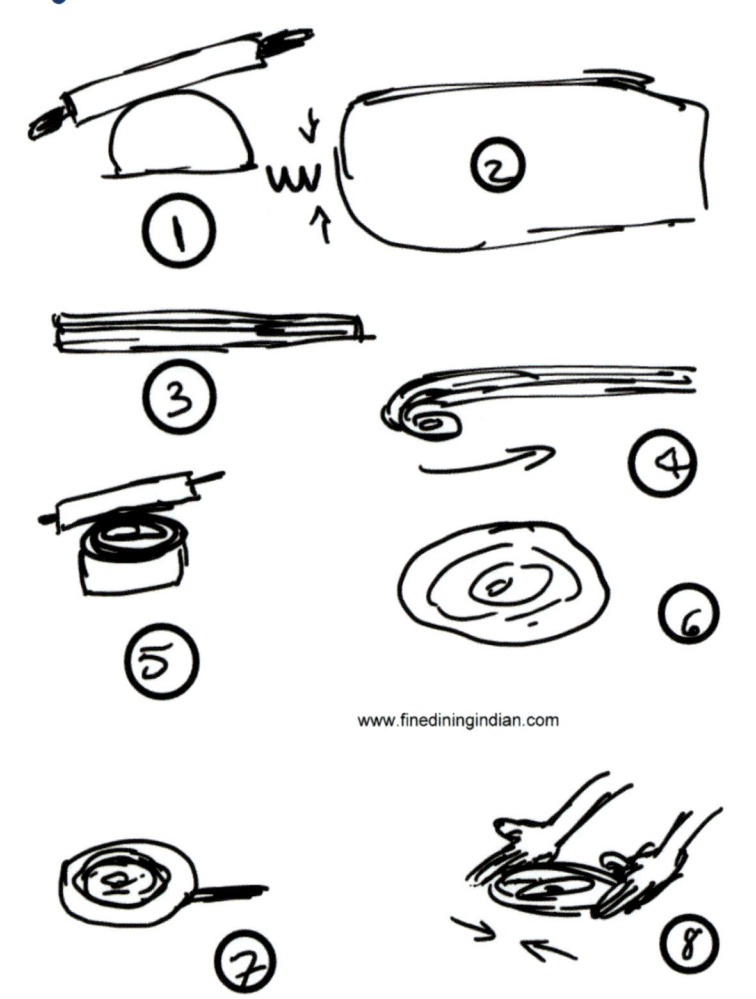

① ② ③ ④ ⑤ ⑥

www.finediningindian.com

⑦ ⑧

Divide the dough into 12 equal pieces approximately 60 g each. Roll into small balls and apply oil on each roll; cover and rest for another 15 minutes.

Flatten each ball as thin as possible, like dough sheets. Use oil instead of flour while rolling.

Apply oil on whole surface and cut the sheet lengthwise in two.

Take one part, folding from one side to the other width-wise as you make a "w" shape with the dough sheet, like a paper fan.

Now roll in the folded sheet lengthwise from one end to other like a spool and tuck the end under the roll so when you flatten the layer will not open up. Hold

This is a very important process to get the layers. Repeat the process with other side and with remaining dough. Cover the spiral rolls and rest for 15 minutes. Preheat a metal griddle or a flat pan.

Apply oil on a marble top using a rolling pin and flatten rolls round with a 0.5cm thickness.

Cook on medium to high heat on each side, smeared with oil, to get golden brown spots and layers to puff up. When cooked properly, you can break using two fingers.

Each porotta takes about 2–3 minutes for cooking. Maintain medium heat throughout to cook evenly without burning.

To get the layers separated, remove porotta from pan, and smear line of oil with a brush. Beat both sides of porotta using the hard surface of your palm in a clapping motion.

Try not to overdo; otherwise, you will end up breaking the porotta into pieces.
Repeat the process for remaining porotta rolls.

Suggestions:

Knead the dough well enough to get good softness and elasticity. Always cook in a medium to high heat so you get the perfect texture ; when the temperature of stove is low the bread gets dry and hard once cooled down.

Flaky bread tossed in chicken curry
(kuthu porotta)

The name Kuthu indicates acts of motion where the cook uses sharp steel spatulas to break and mix the porotta into small, flaky pieces.

Serves: 2
Course: accompany main or teatime snack

200 g chicken curry **(page 63)**
4 plain porotta
30 mL vegetable oil

50 g onion, finely chopped
10 g ginger garlic paste
2 green chilies, thinly sliced
30 g tomato, finely chopped
1 egg
5 g pepper powder
10 g fennel powder
Salt to taste

Break porotta in small pieces and set aside. In a thick-bottomed flat pan, heat oil, add onion, and sauté until onion becomes light brown.

Add ginger and garlic paste and sauté until the raw flavor disappears.
Now add the tomato, green chilies, and curry leaves, and sauté until tomato gets tender. Add the chicken curry. Heat chicken by spreading it and bringing it to the center with a strong, flat spoon.

Beat the egg and add over the cooked chicken pieces. Mix well. Add the crumbled porotta.

Chop further and mix simultaneously using the flat spoon; add pepper, fennel powder, and salt; and check seasoning. Adjust if required.

The dish can be served on its own, or for added fine-dining value, it can be topped with a fried egg—quail, duck, or chicken, according to your service standards.

Suggestions:

Try to keep the mixture moist. If required, add more curry sauce, water, or chicken stock to keep the dish moist and tasty.

The innovation of kuthuporotta can be defined as a brilliant utilization or recycling of leftovers.

You can use the same recipe of chicken wings to make chicken curry with boneless pieces, or flake the wings to get meat without bones. For me, the best part in chicken is the wing meat, as it is sandwiched between bones and is the juiciest part.

This is an excellent dish that can be easily adopted for onsite cooking at any upmarket restaurant. This is a Kerala version of teppanyaki.

Beyond curry by bobby

Steamed Idli savory rice pudding, Dosa pan cake, Traditional breakfast dish of Kerala

Serves: 20–30
Course: accompany main or breakfast dish

50 g black gram lentils, split
200 g white rice
5 g fenugreek seed
Salt to taste

Wash and soak together lentils, rice, and fenugreek overnight or for 5 hours. Drain and wash again; strain without water. Grind it to a very smooth paste by adding just enough water. For best results, use a stone grinder.

Check the consistency by touching the batter; there should be no grainy feel. The batter gets shiny when ground smooth.

Put the batter in a deep container and allow to ferment naturally, keeping it at room temperature. The batter will rise, so you have to choose the correct container, or it will overflow.

When the batter has risen, you can stir and refrigerate it if you want use it later.

Before cooking, take out the required amount and add salt. Adjust consistency by adding water; it should be thick for idli and thin for dosa

It is very important for the batter to be fermented if it is used for idli; otherwise, when you steam idli, it will be very hard. For dosa, it is optional for the batter to ferment.

For idli

Keep the batter to a thick consistency. Grease the idli stand with oil and pour batter in each slot. Steam, covered, until you hear the whistle sound. If the steamer has no whistle, steam for 5–10 minutes. Carefully open the steamer lid without dropping the vapour on cooked idli.

For dosa

Dilute the batter to a pouring consistency. Heat a non-stick, round, flat pan.

Spread the batter in a round shape and cook by turning sides; apply oil on top for color and crispy texture.

When you make thin layers, the dosa will be crispy and thicker for a soft texture.

Crispy and soft rice pancake with fermented rice batter Hoppers (Appam)

"Appams" are a famous breakfast from Kerala. This is a relatively simple recipe, but you may need some practice to perfect it. Also known as hoppers.

Serves: 25–30

Course: accompany main or breakfast dish

250 g raw white rice
50 g cooked rice
200 mL coconut milk
10 g sugar
3 g dry yeast
10 mL lukewarm water
Salt to taste
Oil for cooking

Wash and soak raw white rice for 3–4 hours until it turns bright white. Drain and set aside. Grind raw and cooked rice in a blender with 100 mL coconut milk.

Remove from blender and add remaining coconut milk and salt.

Dilute yeast with lukewarm water and sugar. Allow to proof for 5 minutes, and then add to the rice paste.

Mix well and make sure the batter is of a smooth pouring consistency. Keep covered for another 2–3 hours and allow fermenting.

Before cooking, stir the batter. If it is thick, add milk or water to give it a thin pouring consistency.

Heat an appam pan (a deep, non-stick concave pan) and grease lightly with oil. Pour one big spoon of batter into pan.

Slowly rotate the batter in the pan in a circular motion so that a thin layer forms on the sides while the middle remains thick.

Cover and cook until the middle part becomes fluffy and the edges become golden. Repeat the process with the remaining batter.

Suggestions:

The batter will perform much better and have a fluffy soft inside when made a day before. Check the sugar level in the batter—it should taste slightly higher than the salt level. Sugar promotes the coloring of the thin sides and gives a crunchy feel.

In the lamb masala recipe, we used the appam that is cooked in a flat pan rather than a concave one for presentation purposes.

You are more than welcome to try a different size or shape. The dish is called appam, not the shape.

Sautéed and steamed rice flour cake (Puttu)

Serves: 2
Course: accompany main or breakfast dish

300 g raw rice (white or brown)
50 g fresh grated coconut
Water
Salt to taste

Soak rice in water for 4 hours or until the rice swells and becomes bright white. Drain and grind it to a coarse to fine powder.

Dry sauté rice powder in flat thick-bottom pan on medium heat to remove the raw flavor until dry free flowing texture .

Spread the rice on a flat tray and allow to cool .

Mix rice powder with salt, sprinkle with just enough water to wet the flour, and combine well.

To check the consistency of the mixture, hold a handful to make a tight ball; when you press, it should break freely.

Keep the base of the steamer in hot water and allow to boil.

Place the perforated stainless steel disc in the cylindrical mold. Put a handful of grated coconut on top of the perforated disc, and then add wet rice flour until half full.

Follow with another handful of grated coconut, fill another half with rice flour, and finish with grated coconut on top. Close the lid and steam until you see steam escaping through lid.

Suggestions:

The best results are always when you fill the mold with loosely done mixture with just enough water to combine together when steaming. Also it cooks faster lighter than a mix than sticking to hand an pressed in to the mold.

Beyond curry by bobby

Spiced Lamb and basmati rice biryani cooked in casserole (Lamb biryani)

Serves: 6
Course: main

For the rice

400 g basmati rice
20 g cinnamon
10 g cloves

10 g cardamom
5 g black pepper
Salt to taste

For lamb

500 g lamb, boneless
100 g clarified butter
150 mL neutral oil
250 g onions, sliced
150 g tomatoes, chopped
15 g ginger, sliced
20 g garlic, sliced
6 green chilies
5 g turmeric powder
15 g red chili powder
15 g coriander powder
15 g garam masala powder
15 g fennel powder
1 g saffron
50 mL milk
200 mL yogurt
20 g mint leaves, chopped
15 g coriander leaves, chopped
Salt to taste

Wash rice gently until the water becomes clear. Soak rice for 30 minutes.

Drain and set aside. Heat oil in a heavy-bottomed pan. Add one-fourth of the sliced onions and fry them until they become golden in color and crisp in texture.

Remove the onions in a paper towel and keep for garnish. Clean and cut the lamb into 50 g pieces. Wash and drain well.

Grind the ginger, garlic, and green chilies in a food processor until it becomes a coarse paste.

Heat oil in a thick bottom pan and add remaining sliced onions; fry until it becomes translucent. Add the ginger garlic chili paste and fry for a minute. Add the tomatoes; sauté until softened.

Add all powdered spices; sauté until the oil starts to separate. Add the curd, half of mint leaves, and coriander leaves.

Now add lamb pieces and mix well. Season with salt, pour water or mutton stock until it covers lamb, and cook over low heat until the mutton is tender.

Frequently check to prevent the masala from burning and sticking to the bottom of the pan. If needed, add more water or lamb stock.

The lamb masala should have some thick gravy when cooked.

Boil rice along with all whole spices and salt, until it is 60 per cent cooked.

If you want to discard whole spices, tie them in cheesecloth before adding to water. Drain and reserve rice.

Preheat the oven to 165 °C.

Grease an ovenproof casserole with clarified butter. Spread half of the lamb masala and layer half of the part-cooked rice over it.

Pour 2 tbsp of clarified butter on top and sprinkle some fried onions, mint, and coriander leaves. Repeat the step with remaining rice and lamb.

Spoon around 50 mL saffron-soaked warm milk on top of biryani rice.

Place greaseproof paper over rice and close the lid; bake in the oven for 20 minutes. Check whether rice is cooked but retaining shape. Serve equal amounts of rice and lamb.

Suggestions:

A good biryani must have perfectly cooked lamb and rice. Rice should be free-falling without sticking to serving spoon.

In traditional cooking, half-burned wood pieces are placed on top and bottom of biryani casserole once it's sealed with wet dough, and it's opened only at the time of serving.

Once the dough is cooked, it indicates the biryani is also cooked. You can substitute lamb with other meat, fish, or vegetables.

Boiled and sauted Cassava, Seabass
(Kappa, meen curry)

Tapioca or cassava was the main staple for all farmers in the old days, when they could not afford to buy rice. It was their main source of energy.

Serves: 6
Course: main

For tapioca
500 g diced tapioca/cassava
50 mL coconut oil

3 g mustard seed
50 g grated coconut
5 g cumin seeds
50 g sliced shallots
2 green chilies
10 g garlic pods
1 sprig curry leaves
Salt to taste

For fish curry

400 g sea bass (or any similar oily fish)

Coconut paste

100 g grated coconut
15 g chili powder
10 g coriander powder
3 g turmeric powder

To finish

30 mL coconut oil
1 g fenugreek seed
3 g mustard seeds
20 g garlic, sliced
15 g ginger, sliced
2 sprigs curry leaves
2 slit green chilies
50 g sliced shallots
1 medium-sized tomato, cut in quarters
1 drumstick
50 g cocum(tamarind) soaked in water
200 mL fish stock/water
Salt to taste

For tapioca (kappa)

Boil tapioca pieces and salt with enough water to cover; when half cooked, change water with fresh boiling water and adjust salt. Cook completely until soft. Drain off the excess water.

Grind together grated coconut, chilies, cumin, shallots, and garlic, adding a little water to make a coarse paste.

Heat coconut oil in a pan. Add mustard seeds and curry leaf; allow spluttering. Add the ground paste; sauté for a minute.

Add cooked tapioca pieces and mix well without crushing the pieces, until raw flavor of ingredients vanishes. Adjust seasoning and remove from fire.

For fish curry (meen curry)

Clean, cut , wash, and drain fish.
Grind all ingredients mentioned to a smooth coconut paste.

Take drumstick, scrape skin, wash, and cut into 5-cm long batons, then split all pieces in half by length.

To finish the sauce, heat oil in a thick-bottom saucepan.

Add fenugreek seeds and wait until it turns golden brown, then add ingredients until drumstick one by one, sautéing in between.

Add coconut paste and sauté for a minute. Add fish stock or water and give the sauce one boil; check seasoning. Slide in fish.

Add the remaining curry leaves and soaked cocum with water soaked in. Bring to a boil, remove from heat, cover with a lid, and allow cooking on very low heat. This helps the fish retain amazing texture and flavor.

Check consistency of sauce after 30 minutes to a semi thick pouring stage. Serve with tapioca

Suggestions:

Tapioca gives best taste when it made to semi mash texture; so that the seasoning is perfectly even. The fish recipe you can try with most oily round fish one of the best combination will be Tuna.

Pickles and Condiments

Gunpowder 161
Spiced shrimp powder 162
Coconut chutney 163
Tomato chutney 164
Tamarind chutney   165
Mango pickle 166

Gunpowder (Mulagupodi)
Spicy rice chutney powder

Serves: 5
Course: accompany idli or dosa

200 g white rice
50 g split black lentil
50 g Bengal gram lentil
5 g cumin seeds
20 mL coconut oil
2 g asafetida
6 red chilies
5 g peppercorns
5 g sesame seeds
1 sprig curry leaves
Salt to taste

Dry roast the peppercorn, red chilies, and curry leaves in oil until they change color . Add the remaining ingredients and fry until they turn golden brown.Spread in a flat tray to cool down and powder finely.Store in dry, airtight bottles. When serving with idli or dosa, mix a few spoons of chutney with coconut oil, also be eaten dry as a taste enhancer condiment.

Spiced shrimp powder (Chemmeen chamanthy podi)

Serves: 5

Course: accompany rice or savoury rice porridge

150 g dry prawns
100 g desiccated coconut
5 whole dry red chilies
50 g shallots
20 g garlic, crushed
2 sprigs curry leaves
30 g tamarind
Salt to taste

In a Chinese-style wok or similar pan, dry roast prawns to a golden brown and put aside. In the same pan, dry roast coconut with garlic, shallots, red chili, and curry leaves until the coconut turns golden brown and the curry leaves turn crisp. Use low heat, or else the coconut will start burning but not be crispy. Towards the end of browning, add tamarind and salt to coconut and toss well until the mixture gets hot. Add roasted prawns and check the seasoning; if needed, adjust salt.
Spread in a flat tray, cool, and grind to a powder. Keep in an airtight container at room temperature; it can stay fresh for at least two months.

Coconut chutney (Thenga Chammanthy)

Serves: 5

Course: accompany idli or dosa

For coconut paste
150 g grated coconut
2 whole dry red chilies
30 g sliced shallots
5 g ginger
Salt to taste
1 cup water
For seasoning
30 mL coconut oil
2 g mustard
1 red chilies
1 sprig curry leaves

Grind together coconut, red chilies, ginger, and salt, and add water.

Heat oil in a pan or a kadai. Splutter mustard seeds. Add broken red chilies and curry leaves and sauté for a second. Pour it over the chutney.

Tomato chutney (Thakkali achar)

Serves: 5

Course: accompany idli or dosa

100 g chopped tomato
30 mL oil
2 g asafetida
3 g mustard seeds
1 whole dry red chili
3 g cumin seeds
10 g chopped garlic
30 g chopped shallots
2 g turmeric powder
10 g chili powder
100 mL water
Salt to taste

Heat oil in a saucepan , add asafetida powder, and then mustard seeds. When they start cracking, add cumin seeds, dry red chilis, and garlic. When the red chilies turn brown, add the tomato mixed with turmeric and red chili powder. Sauté until the tomato starts leaving water and sticking to the pan. Add water and cook on low heat until the tomato is cooked to a mash-like texture and the water is fully absorbed.

Tamarind ginger chutney (Puli Ingi)

Serves: 5

Course: accompany sadhya (feast served on banana leaf)

200 g tamarind (puli)
4 green chilies
50 g ginger (Ingi) chopped
200 g jaggery powder (palm)
2 whole red chilies
3 g mustard seeds
2 g red chili powder
20 mL neutral flavored oil
Salt to taste

In a thick bottom saucepan heat oil.

Add mustard seeds. After they start cracking, sauté the whole red chilies, then add the chopped ginger and green chilies and fry for a minute.

Add the tamarind pulp, red chili powder, jaggery, and salt, and cook on low heat until the mixture thickens.

When it gets a coating consistency similar to honey, remove from heat to cool down. If you store it in an airtight container, it can stay fresh for up to two months.

Mango pickle (Manga achar)

Serves: 5

Course: accompany biryani, rice dishes

200 g diced raw mango
15 g red chili powder
5 g asafetida
3 g turmeric powder
2 g mustard seeds
50 mL mustard oil
20 mL distilled malt vinegar
Salt to taste

Crackle mustard seeds in a pan of hot mustard oil.
Remove pan from heat; add chili powder, salt, asafetida, and turmeric. Stir for a few minutes until the spices get a roasted flavor, but be careful not to burn them.
Turn off the heat and let the spices cool down. Add vinegar to this mixture. In a mixing bowl, toss the cut mangoes and spice mixture thoroughly. Transfer to an airtight container and keep safe for three days for the flavor to get infused into mangoes.

A

Aatin karal kurumilagittathu · 107

Aatirachi · 103

Acknowledgments · 6

Appa chatti · 38

Appam · 145

Asafetida · 28

Avial · 117

B

Banana Flower and Stem · 26

beetroot air · 88

Beetroot pachadi · 129

biryani · 150

Black cardamom · 21

Brown Rice · 26

C

Cardamom · 20

Cardamom and lime air · 84

Carrot puree · 104

Casual Dining · 55

Cauliflower emulsion · 84

Cheena chatti · 38

Cheera mezukkupuratty · 128

Chemmeen chamanthy podi · 162

Chemmen varuthathu · 87

Chilies · 23

Cinnamon · 21

Cloves · 21

Coconut · 28

Coconut chutney · 163

Coconut Oil · 30

Colacasia · 27

Copyright · 3

Country chicken curry · 63

Curry Leaf · 24

D

Dedication · 2

Dosa · 142

Drumstick · 29

Drying · 37

F

Fenugreek · 22
Fine Dining · 55
Finediningindian.com · 4
Food Design · 45
Food presentation · 41

G

Gingelly Oil · 31
Gunpowder · 161

I

Idli · 142
Introduction · 7

J

Jackfruit · 29

K

Kadala curry · 120
Kappa · 155

Karimeen · 93
Kerala · 11
Kerala Banana · 26
Kerala cuisine · 11
Kerala porotta · 134
Kokum · 25
koonu ulli theeyal · 123
kopra · 14
kuthu porotta · 139

L

Lateral Arrangement · 43

M

Maatirachi ularthiyathu · 111
Manga achar · 166
Mango pickle · 166
Mappas · 78
Meen curry · 155
Meen molly · 95
Meen vevicathu · 83
Mulagupodi · 161
Mustard Oil · 31

Mustard Seeds · 22

N

Nadan kozhi curry · 63
Njandu · 98

O

Offals · 67
Onam · 12
Onasadhya · 15

P

Payasam · 17
Pearl spot · 93
Pepper · 20
Pickling · 36
Piralan · 99
Pollichathu · 93
Porichathu · 90
Poultry Recipes · 61
Sravu thoran · 71
Pre-Opening · 57
Puli Ingi · 165
Puttu · 148

Puttu steamer · 38

R

Restaurant Service · 54

S

Sadhya · 15
Sambar · 125
Seva nazhi · 38
Shrimp powder · 162
Spice fried idli · 65
Spices · 19
Stacked Style · 44

T

Tamarind · 24
Tamarind ginger chutney · 165
Tapioca · 25
Texture · 48
Thakkali achar · 164
Tharavu · 77
Tharavu mutta pattani thoran · 130

Thenga Chammanthy · 163

Toddy · 30

Tomato chutney · 164

U

Umami · 51

Upma · 108

V

Vegetable stew · 74

Vishu · 13

W

Wood pigeon · 71

Y

Yam · 27

Online Free Resources

E-mail
supriya.premaraj@finediningindian.com

Webpage
www.finediningindian.com

Youtube cooking demonstration
www.youtube.com/user/finediningindian

Facebook
www.facebook.com/1.Finediningindian.com.1

Twitter
www.flickr.com/photos/finediningindian

Google Plus
www.plus.google.com/u/0/116822759630277716760

Flickr
www.flickr.com/photos/finediningindian

Stumbleupon
http://www.stumbleupon.com/stumbler/finediningindian

Our new book in making

Starters by finediningindian.com

Please share the knowledge you gained.
Bobby

Thank you

For

Purchasing the book and supporting
www.finediningindian.com

Printed in Germany
by Amazon Distribution
GmbH, Leipzig